35mm
PHOTOGRAPHY

35mm
PHOTOGRAPHY
ADRIAN BAILEY

**DRAGON'S
WORLD**

To the late Jack Nisberg, photographer, 1922-1980, this book is affectionately dedicated.

ACKNOWLEDGEMENTS

This book would have remained forever undeveloped and unfocused without the encouragement and the invaluable contributions from the following people: Hubert Schaafsma, the publisher, who with commendable patience held at bay seemingly implacable deadlines while I was still taking pictures, writing the text, and making excuses. Julia Hands, Dinah Parkinson and Jonathan Harley of Dragon's World who managed to resolve the unresolvable, and Ian Huebner who helped me to design the book, executed the finer points of the layout, and did the drawings and diagrams. I would also like to thank Jonathan Hilton for editing the text, and my wife who made valuable comments and wondered when it was going to end.

Special thanks are due to the Longroom Studio, who took the studio shots of cameras, equipment, the camera handling sequence, and contributed to the darkroom section in words and pictures. Thanks are also due to photographers Chris Bonington, Hugh Clark, David Evans, John Freeman, John Salmon, and Ariane Nisberg who contributed pictures taken by the late Jack Nisberg; individual picture credits are given on the back page.

A number of companies gave freely of their services and loaned equipment beyond our expectations. These include Canon UK, City Camera Exchange, Johnsons of Hendon (Tamron lenses), Kodak, Leeds Camera Centre of London, Leitz, Nikon UK, Minolta, Olympus, Paterson Products, Pentax, Photax (Contax and Yashica), Photopia International (Ricoh) and the Science Museum of South Kensington, London. Individuals that deserve to be mentioned in dispatches are Jane Harvey of Canon, David Durrans of Kodak, Harry Collins of Nikon, and Paul Thurman of Paterson Products.

I would also like to thank Gerry Porter for lending us a Gullwing Mercedes Benz; Dr. Alan Robinson of Langley Grammar School, Buckinghamshire, for permission to photograph the school Sports Day; The Holiday Inn, Swiss Cottage, for use of their Mandarin Suite as a location; The Hyatt Carlton Tower Hotel, Knightsbridge, for the use of their Belgravia Suite as a location.

Finally, there are those people who patiently stood or sat while I photographed them, often with helpful suggestions: Eric Ambler, Tamara Beckwith, Alan Bennett, Peter Blake, Chris Bradley, Mel Calman, Helen Cave, Len Deighton, Amelia and Sarah Gentleman, Leslie Kenton, Colin and Mary Macpherson, Chris Matthew, Jeremy Menuhin, Stirling Moss, Pippa and Jamie Rubinstein, John Salmon, Julian and Mary Scott, Lilliane Shammas, the Sterling String Quartet, Daisy Wallace, Don Warrington.

Dragon's World Ltd
Limpsfield
Surrey RH8 0DY
Great Britain

© Copyright Dragon's World Ltd 1987

Jacket airbrush illustration: Philip Castle

ISBN 1 85028 030 4

Printed in Italy by G. Canale & C. S.p.A. Turin

Previous page

A subject and style more often associated with larger format cameras than 35mm, this still-life group was shot in daylight on a Pentax Spotmatic and with a 200mm lens, using Ektachrome 200.

CONTENTS

INTRODUCTION

Was there ever an occupation more enthusiastically pursued and universally accessible, a medium more suited to innovation and progress than that of photography? Wherever we may be, photographs have become an intrinsic part of everyday life – as posters, in books and magazines, in newspapers, window displays, information leaflets and brochures – everywhere.

Our appreciation of photography, whether we know it or not, has become finely tuned, due to the high standards achieved by reportage and advertising photographers. Over the past century we have acquired a unique visual education and a universal language, an ability to observe and interpret life through the camera lens and, although we may not grasp the rules of photography's pictorial 'grammar' most of us can recognise a good picture when we see it.

Subtlety and humour In photography the subject is of prime importance, and the way that the photographer draws our attention to it and effectively 'edits' it reflects his skill. There is a world of difference between the photograph taken as a snapshot on holiday, or one of the children for the family album, and a photograph that has involved the photographer in a deliberate, picture-creating act. Photography reveals one man's preoccupation with his surroundings, his involvement and responses to everyday life, and the photograph tells us something about his attitudes and ultimately shows his skill at presenting them.

Good photographs capture the essence of a moment in time, they exploit the particular appeal of a subject with subtlety or perhaps with humour, or invest a seemingly mundane and easily overlooked object with freshness. In this way the experienced photographer makes potential photographers of us all. In other words, we see what he is getting at, and it is within us to achieve comparable results.

Element of surprise The urge to take pictures can be transient, or last a lifetime. The novice is dazzled by the endless prospects of photography, seeing only the limitations of cost of film and processing. The great French photographer Jacques-

Henri Lartigue, on taking his first picture at the age of seven, exclaimed, "This is wonderful . . . I'm going to photograph everything, everything!"

Skill at picture-taking comes gradually, through the regular search for promising material – the effects of light and colour, the balance of shapes, the use of texture and form. Often the image is fugitive, like the shadow cast by a cloud, or the appearance of a rainbow, or a figure dashing by. Of course, the great appeal of photography is its ability to snatch a moment of time forever, and in such fine detail. Time is the third dimension of the photograph. I once heard a photographer say that, for him, the best shots are those that flash past his

train window – too late. Such shots may seem wonderfully promising but results are rarely accurately foreseen – even for professionals there's an element of surprise, a margin of error between observing the scene, taking the photograph, and viewing the final print or slide. "I photograph," said the American photographer Garry Winogrand, slightly tongue-in-cheek, "to find out what something will look like photographed."

Lake Maggiore, Italy (above), in early evening. Taken on a Pentax S2 and 35mm lens, using Ektachrome 200 film. **Young dancer** (left), on Fujichrome 50, by daylight, taken on a Canon T90 and 70mm lens.

Tactile appeal *35mm Photography* covers those subjects most of us regularly encounter, plus those that have become a familiar part of the photographic repertoire. Most of the pictures that follow were taken specifically for this book. One or two were selected from my archives, dusted off, and used to make a point or two. Some were shot decades ago, others were taken yesterday, as it were. Less than a dozen were taken while I was on an assignment for magazines, and the majority were shot in circumstances familiar to every photographer – in the street, in the countryside, in domestic surroundings, hotels, by the sea, by the side of playing fields and racetracks accessible to everyone.

In the main I used medium-speed

slide film in a wide variety of cameras, ranging from an antique Exacta and a Kodak Retina, through to a much-used Pentax Spotmatic and several of the up-to-date models from the big five manufacturers.

Wonderful versatility My intention was to make this book as much a picture book as a manual of photography; I have splashed out on a few big pictures of cameras because, to the keen photographer and the novice alike, cameras are appealing and tactile, and affirm photography's brief but dazzling history of technical progress.

In some respects it is a pity that photography has become an industry. It is unlikely that there will be any more pioneers like Frederick

INTRODUCTION

Scott Archer, who invented the wet plate process, or Mannes and Godowsky who perfected the first tri-pack colour film. But, if the human touch is missing, there is no doubt that only corporate energy and finance could have developed autofocus and computer flash. These were brooks too broad for leaping by any but such industrial giants as Canon, Nikon and Minolta. The progress made with improved films by Kodak, Agfa and Fuji has meant that the end result is practically guaranteed – you can hardly fail to get an acceptable picture since the automatic camera leaves you free to concentrate on the task of picture making.

This book deals with the 35mm camera because of its world-wide popularity – there are about 200 models currently on the market – and its wonderful versatility. Once you have learned the foundation of photography as a visual technique or 'language' you will rapidly progress from pictures that are mere snapshots to photographs in their own right that were worth taking and worth keeping. I believe that anyone who has ever picked up a camera possesses the ability to take good pictures.

Although the subject is the vital element of any picture, the way in which this is presented by judicious use of exposure, focusing, camera position, and other factors, clearly establishes the difference between the casual snapshot and the considered photograph.

Café interior, Hyères, France (previous page), which is now a supermarket. Exposure was about 1/30th sec at f/3.5 with the camera steadied on a table. A Pentax Spotmatic used with a 35mm lens and Ektachrome 200.

Snowscape with figures, Chiltern Hills (right). The grey, wintery atmosphere was maintained by underexposing and letting dark areas dominate. Exposure was about 1/60th sec at f/8 or f/11, on a Pentax Spotmatic and 35mm lens using Ektachrome 100.

35MM

▷ THE IDEAL FORMAT ◁

Lobster boat, Dorset
(opposite) taken by the light of the setting sun, which gave a metallic sheen to the surface of the sea. Nikon FA and tripod with 500mm lens and Agfachrome 100. Exposure was about 1/30th sec at f/8.

Building in Antony, Devon taken on Kodak infrared film. The unnatural colours are due to the unusual characteristics of IR film, in this case used without the customary Wratten 12 IR filter on a Pentax camera.

The camera principally associated with 35mm film is the single lens reflex or SLR – the camera being used in the picture above. SLRs convey the scene being photographed through the lens, via an angled mirror and a glass penta-prism to a glass screen, so the scene through the view-finder is identical to that through the lens. A close rival in popularity to the SLR is the compact camera. Most employ a direct-vision viewfinder window adjacent to the lens – the scene viewed is approximately but not exactly the same as that seen by the lens. Compacts are pocket sized, easy to handle and operate and incorporate many advanced technical features. The camera that started the 35mm trend, the prestigious and expensive Leica, is traditionally of the rangefinder type – although there are SLR Leicas – where sharp focusing is achieved by superimposing a split 'ghost' image.

SMALL IS BEAUTIFUL – BARNACK'S LEICA

The 35mm format, actually 24 x 36mm, was introduced nearly a century ago by Thomas Edison, who devised a celluloid film to fit his cine camera, punching holes in the edges of the film to advance it through the shutter mechanism. Over the past 30 years, the improved quality of colour emulsions, matched by the rapid progress in the design of the SLR camera, has made 35mm the most widely used type of film.

Oscar Barnack, pioneer camera designer and inventor of the Leica.

screen on top of the camera.

Eye-level view The first 35mm single lens reflex camera was the Kine Exacta, made by Jhagee of Dresden in 1935. Early models had a noisy shutter and a flip-up-mirror that caused the screen to go blank when you released the shutter. On top of the camera was a flip-up hood, down which you peered to view the screen.

This was the way things went util Zeiss introduced the Contax S in 1949, which incorporated a penta-prism for eye-level viewing. Cameras now began to expand their range of interchangeable lenses, and innovations accrued rapidly: Pentax developed the instant-return mirror; Yashica the first electronic shutter; and Nikon the first automatic aperture. Topcon launched TTL (through the lens) metering, while Fujica had the first camera with LEDs (light-emitting diodes). The way ahead was marked by Ricoh's autofocus lens of 1980 and, five years later, Minolta introduced the first integral autofocus SLR.

Practically everyone has at some time in their lives handled a camera. "Cameras," wrote the novelist and film maker Susan Sontag, "go with family life." The first popular, mass-produced model was the famous Kodak Brownie of 1900. At five shillings, or one dollar, the Brownie had a fixed-focus lens and a one-speed shutter. What was now needed was a precision-built small camera to appeal to the serious amateur and perhaps the professional, too.

The need had already been anticipated, and in 1905 a German optical designer, Oscar Barnack, imagined a camera that would take a 'small negative' but yield a 'big picture'. The small negative sought by Barnack had for some time been used by the motion picture industry – 35mm film with sprocket holes along the edges.

Legend Barnack designed a slim, lightweight, metal-bodied camera to take the 35mm cine-film, and sold the idea to the microscope manufacturing firm of Leitz in Wetzlar, Germany who made a prototype. It needed a name and Leitz thought 'LECA' would be appropriate (LEitz CAmera). After many modifications the camera was revealed at the Leipzig Fair of 1925: Leca had become 'Leica' – and the Leica became a legend. The camera employed the rangefinder system of focusing, where you adjust the lens until a split image is juxtaposed for sharp focus.

It was a matter of time before someone had the idea of combining the 35mm format with the reflex system, which uses an angled mirror to reflect the image to a viewing

Fine art of 35mm camera design Below the hefty exposure meter is the first 35mm SLR, the Kine Exacta, which is, even today, a pleasure to use. On the book is the rare French 'Le Furet' with a fixed lens and three shutter speeds. Below, the Austrian 'Amourette' took a cassette cartridge and had two aperture settings – f/6.3 and f/11.6. The rangefinder Contax on the far right could be fitted with a tele lens as shown, which made it versatile but heavy. In the centre is an early Leica. The 1950s Contax F, on the left, bears the now familiar pentaprism housing and, like my Pentax Spotmatic below, is a classic camera and well-worn survivor of many years of enjoyable shooting.

THE DEALER'S VIEW CAMERA EXCHANGE

For amateur and professional photographer alike, the photographic dealer buys and sells cameras, handles complaints and gives encouragement. His advice is valuable, his knowledge of equipment profound. Many dealers are experienced photographers in their own right, like Tony Honess and the staff of the City Camera Exchange, Brighton.

"Ninety per cent of our customers are amateurs and over half read the camera magazines, so they are quite knowledgeable about technique. With the fierce competition between manufacturers, the magazines try to remain impartial – and so do we – but if someone asks which is the best of the top five makes – Minolta, Canon, Nikon, Olympus and Pentax," Honess smiles – "but not necessarily in that order, the quality is such that it's hard to judge. We recommend to customers a camera to suit their budget, and the one they like the look of; appearances matter."

Best of everything Conservative photographers remain faithful to one make of camera, but a substantial section of the market was converted to autofocus when, as Honess said, Minolta stole the march on all its competitors with their best selling SLR.

"All in all, the greatest criterion to most customers is the price. While some demand that 'best of everything' image that Leica and Nikon create, most young enthusiasts count the cost and shop around for the most favourable deal. If they are looking for an SLR then I start by showing the customer something like a Practika."

Upward trend The cost of equipment makes people cautious, especially colour film and processing. "Did you know that the average number of films put through a camera is over twelve but under twenty-four a year? This means that a 3-year-old Canon, for example, has had only 40 rolls of film put through it, so on the secondhand market it's virtually mint."

At the City Camera Exchange, enthusiasts are encouraged to discuss problems and to show their pictures. They are guided, up to a point, by the photographic magazines, "But," Honess argues, "the magazines don't do enough to inspire their readers. If a magazine does an article about portraiture, their examples rarely represent the best. You need shots that are going to encourage you to emulate the work of, say, Bob Carlos Clark, or someone like that. Yet standards **are** improving, because of the automation, autofocusing, and simply because there are more people with cameras."

Compact performance "We do our own tests on lenses, so we are able to say to our customers – here are the prints, check for yourself." Honess maintains that this is valuable service now that the trend is towards cameras that have a 'system' of one zoom lens and one body. "Perhaps there will come a time when the traditional SLR will be on a par with compacts, in terms of performance and price. We sell more compacts than SLRs and it seems to be the way manufacturers are heading. We'll see a new breed of customer who is attracted to photography because there is finally the technology that enables them to take the kind of pictures that once seemed beyond them."

CAMERA UNLIMITED THE MODERN SLR

The supremacy of the SLR as a universal camera has recently been challenged by the variety and attractiveness of the compact cameras. Their family snapshot appeal is partly due to their relative cheapness when compared with SLRs, and the fact that they make few demands on the photographer by way of technical knowledge.

In the U.S., some five million compacts are sold against the 2.4 million SLRs. Autofocus and microchip automation for exposure programming have played significant roles in the success of compacts so we cannot evaluate the SLR's supremacy in terms of sales, but in terms of *seriousness*.

The SLR is the enthusiast's camera. It is, in a word, businesslike. To buy one implies a degree of commitment on the part of the owner to learn something about photography – about shutter speeds, and depth of field and filters; about flash techniques and about the focal lengths of lenses.

Wealth of accessories By far the greatest advantage of the SLR is its versatility provided by the range of interchangeable lenses. Changing from one lens to another of different focal length alters the angle of view. While a compact may give you an arms-wide sweep of a mountain range, it won't magnify a faraway peak for close scrutiny. The flexibility of the SLR doesn't end with lenses.

The camera body itself is heir to a 'system', a tempting range of accessories offered by the manufacturers – filters, flash equipment, bellows, motor drives and focusing screens – all with the aim of helping you to make the most of any photographic situation and pictorial opportunity.

Automatic exposure SLRs, and compact cameras, too, take 35mm film, which comes in a cassette ready for loading into the camera (see p. 34). Many cameras now load the film automatically with a motorised film advance and rewind system. Also often included is the DX coding system, pioneered by Kodak, which automatically sets the film speed on the camera, otherwise you set it manually – a camera's metering and exposure system has to relate to the sensitivity of the film you are using.

In an SLR, the built-in exposure

meter assesses the strength of the light reflected back from the subject and entering the camera through the lens (TTL), and then recommends a suitable exposure setting. On some cameras you still set exposure manually, but most modern cameras now take over this function and set exposures automatically.

Leading the way Exposures can either be wholly programmed, where the camera decides the appropriate ratio of aperture and shutter (how much light and for how long) according to the subject and lens in use, or goes halfway towards it – you set the aperture and the camera sets the shutter speed, or vice versa. The type of lens has to be taken into account because a wide-angle lens, for example, will accept more light than a long focus lens. Metering systems have kept pace with automation, some offering

'multipattern' readings that analyse areas of the scene and compute an average, ideal exposure.

Cameras with an all-electronic brain will do almost anything, except make coffee. All you have to do, apart from pressing the shutter button, is to remember to remove the lens cap. Such innovation is encouraged by the many excellent photo journals that keep pace with, and are often in advance of, technology. The manufacturers are driven not just by competitiveness, but by the amateur market that leads the way, confirming by their enthusiastic response the wisdom of Minolta's lead in autofocus, the computerised magic-metering of Olympus's OM4, OM40 and Nikon's FA cameras, and Canon's mighty 'Wurlitzer', do-everything camera, the revolutionary T90, shown opposite.

Canon T90, the most advanced and 35mm SLR yet designed.

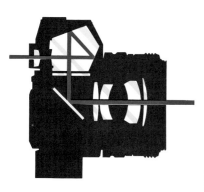

Every camera lens produces an inverted, laterally reversed image. The pentaprism of an SLR corrects this, as light passes through the lens by way of a 45° mirror, through the prism to the viewfinder. When you release the shutter, the mirror flips up simultaneously with the opening of the shutter.

OPTICAL EXTRAS   WHICH CAMERA?

The five cameras pictured below represent a selection from the 70 or more SLRs currently available. The choice was not entirely random – each camera has its own particular features; indeed, every camera on the market has, in some way or other, a claim to your attention.

At the top is the Leica R4. There are not many novice photographers who are prepared to spend over £1,000 on a camera, even though a Leica will probably last a lifetime and represents a good investment. The R4 is fully automatic, but with a manual override option, and has selective metering. As the other four cameras shown here offer similar automation, what is so special about the Leica? Well, with the name Leica you are buying prestige, tradition, dependability and, in a word, class.

Next, moving clockwise, is the Ricoh XR 20SP, about one-fifth the price of the Leica. The Ricoh has a multiprogramme exposure system, which, far from confusing the photographer, is designed to make picture-taking as simple as possible.

Next is the Nikon F-501 AF, a more advanced and autofocus camera with the Nikon pedigree (see also pp. 22-5).

Moving round brings us to an SLR excellent for beginners, the Pentax P30, slightly cheaper than the Ricoh and, by its simplicity, maintaining the fine tradition set by the Pentax Spotmatic (opposite).

Finally, we come to the Olympus OM40, at a price halfway between the Ricoh and the Nikon, and like those two cameras there's an emphasis on the exposure metering. The OM40's 'ESP' (Electro-Selective Pattern) can analyse high-contrast and backlit subjects by computing the various strengths of light for an ideal exposure.

All the cameras below have manual film-advance levers and manual rewind, except for Nikon's motorised advance. The familiar aspects of the standard SLR are gradually giving way to sleeker cameras with no aperture rings, shutter speed dials or film wind levers. Just a button or two, and an LCD (liquid crystal display) panel to give you all the information you need. Will all this make you a better photographer? Probably, but it is worthwhile experiencing the sometimes quirky characteristics of a conventional, manual camera, in case you miss the fun.

Classic controls – viewing screen (right) and top-plate of Pentax Spotmatic 11 (far right). Match needle display: needle is dead centre for recommended exposure, and moves up or down to indicate over- or underexposure. Manual film advance lever, ASA film speed setting, shutter control and frame counter. Manual film rewind. Cable release socket.

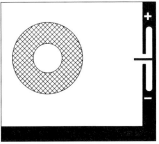

Beginner's SLR – the Pentax P30. Lever advance, manual rewind and shutter speed control retained. Shutter button now incorporated in speed selector dial. AE (automatic exposure) programme and manual exposure modes. DX coding. Viewfinder has split screen and fresnel focusing, and LED exposure display. No cable release socket.

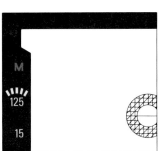

Advanced metering – the Olympus OM4. Multi-spot metering takes up to eight readings from selected parts of the scene and integrates them for the best suitable exposure. Highlight and shadow control, manual film advance and rewind, LCD displays in viewfinder, split screen and microprism focusing display.

True to type – Nikon's F-501 autofocus retains traditional lens mount to take current Nikkor lenses in addition to AF lenses. Auto film advance, but manual rewind. DX coding, three programme modes, aperture-priority AE, auto exposure and auto focus lock, remote control terminal. Exposure LEDs in viewfinder.

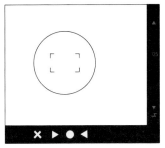

Original autofocus – Minolta 7000, the first SLR to have autofocusing built into the body of the camera. Square-cut purposeful design, it has an LCD display panel on top-plate, plus mode selector buttons. Auto film advance and rewind, auto film loading and DX coding. LED display.

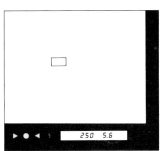

Breaking the mould – the all-purpose Canon T90. Unique body styling, advanced hi-tech, push-button automation: dial-in exposure programming; multi-programme (seven) exposure choice, plus manual, motorised film advance and rewind, built-in 4fps (frames per second) motordrive and multi-metering system.

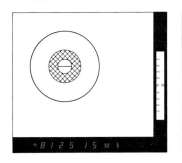

SHARPSHOOTERS AUTOFOCUS CAMERAS

Switch on an autofocus SLR and gently press the shutter release. The response is instantaneous and reassuring. The camera seems to come alive in your hands as the lens begins to buzz and spin urgently until the subject is in focus. Focusing is faster than you or I can say "lens" and much quicker than we can focus manually. This, as you can imagine, is a great advantage when shooting moving subjects, or when you are squinting through a wide-angle lens, where focusing is normally difficult.

Konica introduced the first autofocus camera in 1977 – the C35 compact – and Canon caught up two years later with their now classic Sureshot. Ricoh then produced an AF lens for SLRs in 1980, and the way ahead was suddenly clear.

Wizardry Not a few photographers were sceptical, yet when Minolta's superbly functional 7000 appeared in 1985 the camera became a worldwide bestseller. A camera packed with all the electronic wizardry we had come to expect in SLRs, **and** autofocus thrown in, proved irresistible to over 2 million buyers.

How it works There are two types of autofocus system, the active and the passive. Active systems are used on compacts and on the flash units of autofocus SLRs. Compacts transmit a beam of infrared light to scan the field of view. The lens, linked to the scanner, moves forward towards the infinity setting. When the beam locates a centrally-placed subject and records the maximum of reflected infrared, it is picked up by a cell in the camera. The lens then stops its forward movement and the shutter is released.

SLRs use a passive, phase detection system that analyses the image arriving through the lens. Broadly speaking, phase detection compares areas of contrast in the image, received by a series of detectors at the focal plane. The point of sharpest focus is reached when contrast is at its maximum.

Problems inherent with this system are that the camera is unable to focus on low-contrast subjects and ones in very low levels of light, when you have to fall back on manual focusing.

Even so, the manufacturers – with customary ingenuity – are constantly improving their cameras with

Top: Olympus OM707AF Closest yet to a complete SLR, it has flash built into handgrip.

Centre: Nikon F-501 AF The lens mount is compatible with all Nikkor AI lenses.

Bottom: Minolta 7000 AF The best-seller that started a revolution.

innovations that are soon taken for granted, such as Canon's EOS 650 which can set the depth of field (an increased zone of sharp focus) and the exposure, automatically. To obtain maximum depth of field, you can focus on the background, and press the shutter button halfway – this factor is registered by the camera's computer. You then focus on the foreground, press the button and the information is relayed to the lens, which focuses and stops the aperture down to give you a depth of field covering both extremes. Focus twice on the foreground and the camera will give you *minimum* depth of field. The reluctance of AF cameras to focus in low levels of light is hardly a drawback when you consider how few are the occasions when you need to shoot in the near dark. In fact, Canon's EOS 650, with its ultrasensitive phase detection system will focus in conditions as low

AF focusing is fast. At the peak of the action with the camera on single-servo mode, the lens focuses in an instant and the shutter fires when – and only when – the image is sharp. Focus then stays locked in this position. On continuous servo, focusing readjusts continually with moving subjects. **Panning** with a Nikon F-501, I was able to catch this supersonic RAF Jaguar (below) in sharp focus, even though light was fading.

AUTOFOCUS CAMERAS

as EV1 – this Exposure Value is equal to an exposure of about 1 second at f/2, when you could probably just about discern your hand in front of your face!

When it gets too dark, AF flash takes over, transmitting infrared radiation in a contrasting pattern on the subject, and giving the contrast-based system something to work on. Thus, an AF camera can focus in total darkness. The versatility and value of AF systems is now so well established that every major manufacturer has developed an autofocus SLR, and independent lens makers include a wide range of AF lenses in their lists. Autofocus is no longer an innovation, but an established fact of life.

Recent additions to the autofocus range are the Pentax SFX, with integral TTL auto flash, and the Yashica 230-AF with its unique 'Trap Focus' mode. You can switch to continuous servo for subjects like the racehorses, below, or use the Trap Focus: you prefocus on a selected spot and, when the subject arrives in the zone of sharp focus, the camera automatically fires. AF cameras have both a focusing and an exposure lock. keeping your finger on the AF lock holds the subject in focus (right), allowing you to alter the composition, (bottom right). To shoot an off-centre, backlit subject, take an exposure reading for the subject, use the AE lock, the recompose your picture.

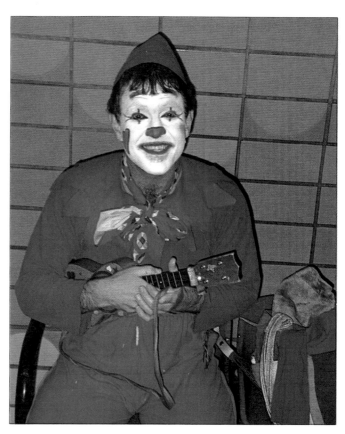

Autofocus flash units on SLRs transmit a pattern of contrasting infrared waves for the benefit of the contrast-based focusing system in the camera. Completion of focusing triggers the flash.

London Underground buskers by flash (right) and natural light (below). Autofocus cameras will work in low light levels, but fail in exceptionally poor light, such as EV 4 to EV 1.

SILENT SERVICE   RANGEFINDER CAMERAS

There is only one 35mm rangefinder camera, apart from one or two compacts, and that is the Leica M4-P, and the M6, identical but for a built-in exposure meter. The rangefinder works by comparing two images of the subject reflected by adjustable mirrors. As you focus the lens, the images move together; when they are aligned the subject is in focus.

Since you do not view the subject through the lens, but through a viewfinder, there is a slight discrepancy between the viewed image and the image recorded on the film – a condition known as 'parallax error'. The viewfinder, however, gives a bright image, and rapid focusing is possible, in poor light which has made the Leica the favourite tool of many professional photojournalists. The shot below, of Edith Piaf's last concert, was made by Vogue photographer Jack Nisberg on a Leica M2 with Kodak Tri-X film.

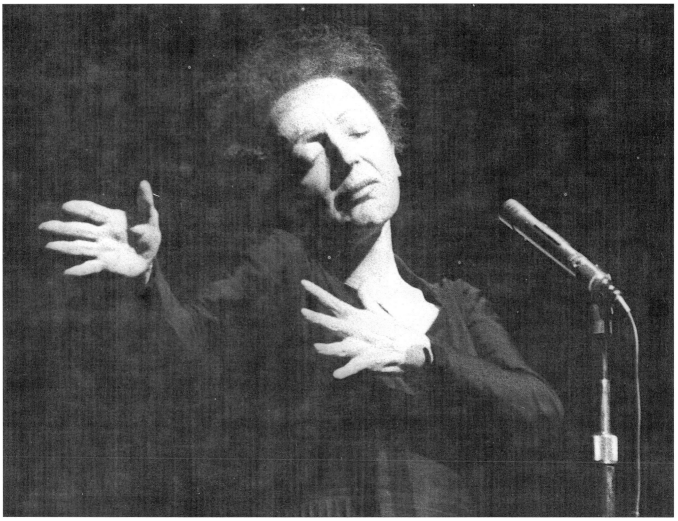

POINT, PRESS AND PRINT –
▷ COMPACT CAMERAS ◁

Handle a compact camera, take pictures with one, and you will find that they are versatile and almost foolproof – some are even waterproof! Because they yield such good results for owners possessing little knowledge of photographic techniques, they have become labelled as 'family' cameras. Yet compacts are used by professional photographers, so do not be misled into thinking that they are mere snapshot cameras – most are dependable and, even in seemingly demanding situations, are capable of producing excellent photographs. In this respect, compacts are descended from the mass-produced and legendary Kodak 'Brownie', the first universal 'point-and-shoot' camera. While the Brownie was not exactly foolproof, its designer hoped to make picture-taking as simple as possible, an achievement maintained by today's designers who have created precision-built compact cameras of high quality.

COMPACT CAMERAS

Lightweight and neatly designed, compact cameras manage to incorporate a host of valuable features in a slimline body. These include automatic metering and exposure, autofocus, integral flash, a self timer, motorised film advance and rewind and auto speed setting with DX-coded films. The high-quality lenses, which in some models can be switched from wide-angle to close-up, have excellent resolution, while shutter speeds range, typically, from 1/8th to 1/500th second.

Compacts are functional and, in their own way, versatile, since they can so easily be slipped into the pocket and are handy for spontaneous shooting. Some, like the Minox, are high-precision miniature cameras that are capable of remarkable definition. From the budget-priced Konicas to the more expensive Canon and Contax cameras, all have managed to cram an attractive, and now it seems essential, range of features in a slimline body.

Exposure metering is extremely accurate, shutter speeds range from 1/8th second to 1/500th in some models (Canon's Sureshot Tele); 1/45th to 1/1000th (Chinon Auto 1001); while budget-priced compacts give you a range from around 1/80th to 1/400th second. Apertures can be as wide as f/2.8 and will stop down to f/27.

Twin-lens and zoom compacts
These allow a choice of focal lengths and therefore different angles of view, give you the chance to move in close to your subject, to crop selectively and reduce depth of field (see also pp. 42-6). You can, with a bit of juggling, hold a telescope or the eyepiece of binoculars to the lens of a compact and get a reasonable telephoto effect (see p. 86).

The electromagnetic shutter blades in some compacts also serve as the diaphragm, and give priority to the aperture. This means that in low light the aperture will widen to allow more light to reach the film, but the shutter speed stays at about 1/125th second. As light levels become lower, and the aperture is at its maximum, the shutter starts to slow down until flash is recommended by an audio signal or a winking LED.

Some compacts, such as Minolta's AF-Z, have selective metering where the spot meter concentrates on the centre of the image to give centre or 'subject-weighted' metering. An exposure lock is a useful feature found on many compacts where you can point the lens at a mid-tone area,

Nikon L35AF2
autofocus is completely automatic, with built-in flash, DX coding and motorised film wind.

Contax T has rangefinder focusing, dedicated clip-on flash and a f/2.8, 38mm Sonnar T lens. High style and expensive.

Minox ML is tiny but a beautifully made camera from the makers of the Leica. Focusing scale, programmed exposure.

Canon AS-6
is an all-weather, showerproof 'adventure' camera. AE program, built-in flash and motor wind.

Kodak 35 AF2 has autofocus, autoflash, DX coding, AE Program, and motor wind. Excellent compact designed by Kodak, made by Chinon.

Canon Sureshot Supreme. Fully automatic stylish compact.

such as the foreground in a landscape, let the meter record this mean exposure level, then press the exposure lock and recompose the picture to include the lighter and darker tones in the scene.

In situations where your subject is against the light, a backlight control on a compact will take into account the extra exposure needed (see also Exposure) and give one stop over. Compact cameras seem particularly tolerant, even in demanding conditions, of strong light and contrast, such as snow scenes and subjects illuminated by bright sunshine, and even where conditions are so dull that it hardly seems worth bothering about – the picture on pages 80-1

was made with a Canon Sureshot where the light on Christmas morning was particularly gloomy.

Integral flash Designed primarily for a huge amateur market (around 16 million manufactured each year), compact cameras also appeal to professional photographers, who use them as a sort of 'visual notebook'. The Minox and Contax T are so versatile, returning a performance comparable with many SLRs, that they are bought by pro's who value them not

Compact cameras are ideal for family snapshots, especially outdoor scenes (below). They also cope very well with tricky lighting situations and extremes of contrast (right).

only for high-precision compactness, but for the high optical standards and advanced automation. The advantages of integral flash is, of course, the reason for the compact's edge over most SLRs, allowing 'fill-in' light for contrasty subjects, and automatically taking over when light levels fall. Both Minox and Contax take dedicated, clip-on flash units while retaining compactness; the majority of other makes has flash built in to the camera body.

Home made filters Why do makers of compacts ignore filters? Canon have included a soft-focus filter in their Supreme Tele, and a thread for a 40.5mm filter, but they are alone in the field, with the exception of Nikon's AF3. A filter can extend the versatility of your camera especially when shooting with a black and white film – an orange or red filter will give a dramatic increase in contrast. I have taped a polarising filter to mine, and you can easily hold a standard-size filter, such as a 49mm or 52mm, over the lens, provided that you don't block the autofocus windows, but your filter must cover the tiny light measuring cell adjacent to the lens, to take into account the extra exposure needed (filters absorb light). If you cannot tape a screw thread filter to your compact, use gelatin filters cut to size, and taped on. A neutral density filter reduces light and makes the aperture open wide. What happens then is that the background is blurred, giving emphasis to subjects in the foreground. With a twin-lens or zoom compact on the 70mm setting, plus a polarising or ND filter, depth of field is further reduced, as in the picture on page 29. Faced with a comprehensive display of the latest compact range (over 125 models!) the prospective buyer is overwhelmed by styling and specification. Developments come thick and fast: after the innovative Minolta company launched the first twin-lens compact, the AF-T, several manufacturers confirmed the trend with their versions, among them Fuji, Konica, Ricoh and Olympus, before Pentax came up with the tele zoom.

Edging closer and closer towards

Twin-lens and zoom compacts (below). Canon Sureshot Tele has two focal lengths, 40mm and 70mm. Pentax zoom covers all focal lengths between 35mm and 70mm, plus macro. The wide-angle (35-40mm) covers a generous area of the scene (right). **Camden Lock** (bottom right and far right) compares extremes of the range.

the versatility of SLRs, Fuji, Konica and Ricoh between them introduced the LCD top plate, fill-in flash, back-light control, drop-in cassette loading, and continuous film drive. Advanced compacts also offer the advantages of finer focusing. Auto-focus systems attain image sharpness by focusing zones or stages, from the simple two-stage budget models, to the 18 stages of the Pentax zoom, and the stepless focusing of the Nikon L35 TWAF. Modest compacts cannot focus closer than a meter or more from the lens, so out-of-focus close up shots are a recurring problem. Cameras with a generous range of stages, however, allow fine focusing from under a meter to infinity.

Built-in flash is useful for night shots (right), and as a fill-in when existing light is too low. Canon's Sureshot Tele incorporates a soft-focus filter for portraits; it also serves to soften cast shadows.

WATERSPORTS ALL WEATHER COMPACTS

Compacts are tough and sturdy little cameras with 'sporty' specifications. I know a mountaineer who carries an Olympus rangefinder XA in his pocket and shoots pictures while balancing on his crampons. Fuji's HD-M all-weather compact is designed for use with gloved hands, and is suitable for skiers. It is also sand and splash-proof, and is one of a number of 'knockabout' water-resistant compacts such as Nikon's LW L35AWAF and the Canon AS-6, featured above.

All three cameras can be taken under water, the Fuji and Nikon are guaranteed to depths of 2 meters (6½ft) and 3 meters (10ft) respectively, while you can take Canon's AS-6 down to 10 meters (33ft). This may seem a considerable discrepancy, but the Fuji and Nikon are primarily all-weather cameras, while the Canon is designed for underwater shooting; you could probably take the Fuji and Nikon deeper, but not under guarantee.

Fuji has manual focus, with zone symbols visible in the viewfinder, the

Pool shots are easy with a watersport compact when you use flash to catch the spray and the action, shot here with the Canon AS-6 on Ektachrome 100 film.

Nikon has auto-focus with manual override (infrared AF systems won't work under water), and Canon is fixed focus, sharp from 1.5 to infinity. All cameras have medium wide-angle lenses, are fully automatic with motorised film wind and built-in flash. The Nikon's f/2.8 35mm lens is protected by a glass cover; the Fuji has a f/2.8 36mm lens, and the Canon an f/4.5 35mm lens.

These wide-angle lenses give emphasis to the appearance of depth, and since water magnifies, a

35mm lens has an effective focal length of about 50mm. The rule when shooting under water is to get as close as possible to your subject; a blue cast prevails and increases with distance. The AS-6 has an accessory frame and a sports viewfinder that can be clipped on to the camera body, plus a close-up lens and distance measuring probe that can be clipped on to the frame.

2

WORKING BRIEF –
▷ CAMERA CONTROLS ◁

It can take a while to become thoroughly familiar with a camera, until operation is as comfortable as putting on an old glove. The optical manufacturers Asahi, who make the Pentax, used to advertise their Spotmatic camera with the slogan 'Just Hold a Pentax', to encourage a personal rapport with the product, and create the concept that handling a Pentax is a rewarding experience. The feel, balance and handling qualities of your camera are valuable aids in establishing confidence, and help to eliminate errors when taking pictures. Loading the film, setting the aperture and shutter speed, focusing, composing the picture, pressing the button, winding on the film and unloading the cassette when the film is finished, all contribute to the eventual success of your pictures and to the enjoyment of photography.

CAMERA CONTROLS

Although the trend is towards automation, where the camera does the thinking, of the 70 or so SLRs available only a dozen, for example, have an integral motor to advance and rewind the film. The classic SLR with its manual controls, such as the Nikon below, is still the most commonly used type, not to mention the wealth of secondhand cameras in circulation. The sequence of pictures that follows explains the various steps in handling a modern SLR camera.

Although cameras are discussed throughout this book, a brief outline of the workings of a modern SLR will help you to familiarise yourself with the principal features. The step-by-step guide on these pages shows the controls of a manual camera, and while the trend with all cameras is now towards automation, handling a do-it-all-yourself camera is like practising five-finger exercises: it gives a firm appreciation of the fundamentals of the discipline.

Anyway, manual control is often necessary, particularly with the aperture and shutter, so manual override on automatic cameras is a vital feature. I cannot deny that automation scores many points over tradition: motorised film advance and rewind is infinitely preferable to the slow, lever wind, which is inclined to jam. It has its darker side, though. I have a Nikon that automatically advances the film but has to be manually rewound. Fine, except that I sometimes forget it's manual and, thinking that the film is safely rewound back into the cassette by the motor, I open the back of the camera . . .

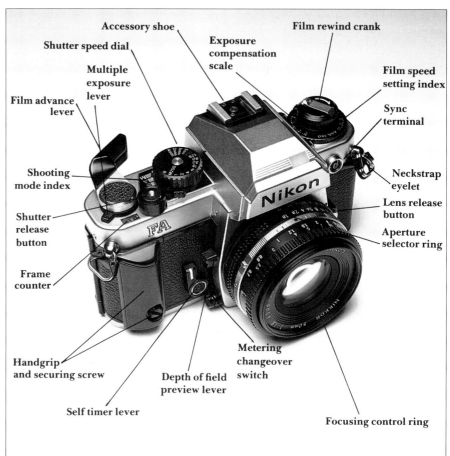

To open the back, cameras employ a wide variety of open/close mechanisms. Nikon's is opened by lifting the rewind knob, but others have slide catches on the back edge. Slip the cassette into the recess so that it fits snugly.

To open the back, cameras employ a wide variety of open/close mechanisms. Nikon's is opened by lifting the rewind knob, but others have slide catches on the back edge. Slip the cassette into the recess so that it fits snugly.

Pull out the film leader to reach the take-up spool. Avoid loading film in direct light. Make sure film compartment is free of grit and dust. Feed the leader well into the slot on the take-up spool.

Start to wind on the film using the film advance lever – you may have to press the shutter button to release the lever. See that the sprocket holes on both edges of the film engage with the sprocket teeth.

Close the camera back, making sure that it has firmly clicked into place. Press down rewind knob. If you accidentally open the camera while shooting, or forget that the camera is loaded, you will fog the film.

Tension the film with the rewind lever to make sure that it isn't slipping on the take-up spool, especially if you have loaded the film in a hurry. Many shots have been lost through the film not winding on.

Activate the wind-on lever until the number one is displayed in the frame counter. You may have to press the shutter button to free the lever, since the action of winding on also tensions the shutter curtain.

Set the film speed. On most manual cameras this is a lift-and-turn ring. Turn it until the number reaches the marker. For example, if your film speed is 100 ISO (or ASA) set this number on the ring.

Set the shutter speed when you have determined the exposure. The dial may also be lift-and-turn, or may have a catch release. Dial is marked B (open shutter) and then from the slowest to the fastest speeds.

Set the aperture on the lens. At f/1.4 the aperture diaphragm is wide open, and at f/16 or f/22 is reduced to its maximum. Lens on an auto program camera may be marked 'A' for automatic operation.

Adjust focus using the focusing ring on the lens barrel. You'll need to familiarise yourself with the lens controls, since aperture control and focusing are closely adjacent. Some zoom lenses have an additional twist ring.

Check depth of field if your camera has a preview button. This shows you how much of the scene is in focus at your set aperture. Having composed your picture, press the shutter button, and wind on the next frame.

Changing the lens during shooting is possible because the shutter prevents light reaching the film. Most cameras have a bayonet mount. After exposing, rewind the film while keeping the rewind button down.

PHOTO FIT—ACCESSORIES

The most essential accessory is a tripod. There are times when you simply cannot get a picture without one—in poor light, with slow film or when using a heavy lens a tripod will prevent camera shake. Ideally, a tripod should be sturdy enough to support the camera and keep it rock steady, and while it may be tempting to choose a lightweight and easily portable model, remember that the entire purpose of a tripod is to keep the camera absolutely still, and as a support for long exposures. The tubular Slik (below, left) is fairly sturdy, while the box-girder, snap-clasp tripod on the right is fast to erect but would benefit from being heavier. Many photographers carry a stout bag which they fill with ballast and hang from the centre post to give the tripod additional stability. The multi-jointed Benbo in the foreground below, is extremely flexible, weatherproof and finished in black to prevent reflections, a feature that will appeal to wildlife photographers. Tripods with a pan-and-tilt facility have a twist grip arm that tightens or releases the tripod head. These have an inherent defect, however, when you are using long-focus lenses: if you fail to tighten the head properly, the lens falls forward on to one of the legs and can dent the edge of the lens barrel or lens hood, possibly damaging the filter thread. An alternative to a tripod is the choice of many sports photographers—the monopod. This will keep a heavy tele lens steady if you brace your legs as additional supports, and use a cable release to fire the shutter. Remote control cables and releases are a further precaution against camera shake.

Other useful accessories include protective front and rear lens caps, and camera body caps. If you find focusing difficult, you may need a correction lens, available in a variety or prescriptions, that fits into a rubber mounting on the eyepiece. Always carry a spare set of batteries, and a changing bag if your camera bag doesn't include one. Changing bags enable you to load and unload film in daylight, for ultra-sensitive IR film, for example, or if your camera jams and you need to open the back to free the film. If you plan to photograph in crowds—such as at a race track—take a lightweight set of steps, preferably with an upper bar to hold on to and to act as an anchor for a camera clamp. A roll of adhesive tape, scissors and a notebook are worth packing, along with a range of filters with appropriate lens thread sizes: polarising, neutral density, colour correcting and compensating filters if you use slide film.

Keep your equipment clean, and lenses free of dust and smears. Carry a puffer brush, and an anti-static cloth to clean your lenses. Some photographers keep their lenses wrapped in plastic bags, others use lens cases, or squares of soft cloth to keep them separate in the accessory bag or carrying case. Ideally, you should travel light, with a minimum of equipment. Accessories can be tempting when displayed in a camera shop, but ask yourself before you buy—'will it contribute towards better pictures?'

VIEWING

 AND FOCUSING ◁

By looking through the viewfinder of your camera you can focus, check the exposure and compose your picture—the viewfinder is the main source of information as well as a source of inspiration. It is here that pictures are made, the film is merely the final record of your judgement. The view seen on the focusing screen of your SLR or through the window of your compact, repays careful study. Whenever possible, take your time, if not by pre-planning the shot, then by observation, taking into account such pitfalls as confused backgrounds, sloping horizons, harsh shadows, and glaring highlights. Nine times out of ten the subject you are photographing should be in sharp focus, though there are occasions when a slightly out-of-focus picture is better than no picture at all.

VIEWING AND FOCUSING

Your viewfinder will display a bright, clear view of the scene. The angle of view—how much of the scene appears in the viewfinder—depends on the lens in use. A zoom lens will give you a view of almost infinite variety. The lens of a compact camera has plenty of scope with a broad view of about 60°. If yours is a manual-focus SLR, focus carefully on the most important part of the main subject.

The standard viewing screen of any 35mm camera is a bright, translucent rectangle the same format as the film. To aid focusing, screens have a central circle enclosing a split-image rangefinder, or a microprism, or both. With a 50mm standard lens fitted to your camera, focusing is straightforward, but wide-angle lenses are less easy to focus because the subject appears further away and the split image device is smaller. With long-focus lenses the zone of focus is shallow and accurate focusing critical. With a standard lens you can focus as closely as 45–50cm (18–20in). At this range everything in the background is blurred even at the smallest aperture, and only the immediate foreground is in sharp focus, so there's little room for manoeuvre. If you now rack the lens back to focus at infinity, the foreground goes out of focus and the background is now rendered sharp. You can use this selective, or differential, focusing to emphasise one part of the picture: throwing one part of the picture out of focus leads the eye to those parts in focus. Selective focusing is governed by camera-to-subject distance, the type of lens and the aperture. When you narrow the diaphragm, an extended zone of focus is created. This zone is called the depth of field.

A

B

C

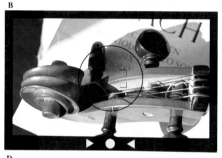

D

Manual focusing cameras have a split image on the viewing screen (**A & B**). Focus is attained when image halves coincide. **Autofocus** cameras use LEDs and audio signals: red arrows and dot turn green and a signal bleeps when subject is in focus (**C & D**). **Compact cameras** have a bright frame Albada finder, and central autofocus spot (**E**). The camera won't fire until the subject is in focus.

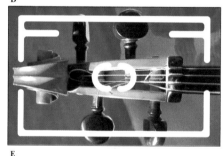

E

Compact viewfinders have a parallax correction frame (right). This is because the viewing window has a slightly different viewpoint to that of the camera lens. The discrepancy is increased in close-up shots, so you need to keep the subject within the framing lines—not as shown here, where you might crop off the subject's nose. As a rule, you should move in close for protraits—but not too close otherwise the image will become distorted (far right).

Familiar faults Low viewpoint (top left) and a wide-angle lens makes buildings appear to fall backwards. Try for a more suitable position. **Careful**, unhurried composing and a lower camera angle would have included the boy's feet (above). **The figure** (left) is vertical, but the horizon is sloping. Keep the camera level.

A fine display of faults Harsh light (below) produces unflattering facial shadows. Use of a lens hood would have prevented patches of flare. Also, there is too much confusing background in relation to the figure, and a tree is growing out of the subject's head, emphasised by her hair style.

VIEWING AND FOCUSING

Selective or differential focusing shifts emphasis within the subject area, depending on the lens type, the aperture, and subject-to-camera distance. Here, a 50mm standard lens and wide aperture creates shallow focus. In the first three pictures, focusing on one figure makes others blurred.

Taking several paces back brings everything into focus. **Moving forward again**, and focusing of girl in front throws her companions out of focus (bottom left). But when you stop down the aperture (bottom right), zone of focus is extended – this is the **depth of field**.

APERTURE
AND DEPTH

The function of the camera lens is to form a visible image and to convey that image to the film. But film is sensitive to light, so you need to vary the brightness of the image by means of a diaphragm—opening up in weak light and closing, or 'stopping down', in strong light. Narrowing this aperture also concentrates the image both in depth and definition: you can actually take a picture without a lens if you 'squeeze' the lightwaves through a tiny hole, pierced through a thin metal plate with a needle. I taped a pierced metal disc over the lens mount of a Nikon SLR and made the picture above in sunlight. The needle-point hole was sufficient to produce a characteristically soft-focus shot, using ISO 100 film, at ⅛th second.

APERTURE AND DEPTH

The aperture diaphragm is calibrated in 'f stops', which usually range from 2, through 2.8, 4, 5.6, 8, 11, 16, 22. The numbers increase as you stop down. At f2 the diaphragm is wide open and at f22 it is at its smallest. By selecting the right aperture you can give depth to a scene or eliminate an intrusive background; it can turn day into night, add richness to colour and balance to the tonal range. Also, by altering the aperture you can create subtle changes of atmosphere in your pictures.

Daylight, natural light from the sun (known to photography as ambient or incident light) arrives in the form of lightwaves, which are either absorbed and/or reflected by those objects they illuminate. The image of a building, for example, is composed of reflected light of various wavelengths and frequencies, which determine the colours in the scene. Short waves form the blue end of the spectrum, long waves the red end, and all wavelengths together make 'white light'. The function of the camera lens is to form a visible image from these lightwaves, and to transmit the image to the film. Because the film is sensitive to light you need to vary the intensity of the image (using the aperture), and also the time that the light acts on the film (using the shutter).

Exposure This is achieved by varying the size of the aperture diaphragm in the lens in relation to the length of time the shutter remains open. The diaphragm controls the passage of the light rays, while the shutter opens and closes for a calculated period, usually fractions of a second.

Angle of view Typically, a camera comes fitted with a 'standard', or normal, lens—a general-purpose lens that approximates the angle of view taken in by the human eye. Such a lens usually has a wide maximum aperture, meaning that it is able to pass the optimum amount of light. You need wide apertures when shooting in weak light, to give selective focus or when you want a fast shutter speed—we'll come to this aperture/shutter relationship

Progressively narrowing the aperture, or 'stopping down', while keeping the same shutter speed, reduces the light reaching the film (above). **Half a stop** or a whole stop under the recommended exposure will enrich colours (especially with slide film) and emphasises highlights and contrast (above centre and right).

f/2.8

f/3.5

f/5.6

f/8

f/11

f/16

shortly.

The aperture diaphragm is regulated by a scale of 'f stops', inscribed on the aperture ring, and each stop either halves or doubles the amount of light reaching the shutter. The stops on a standard lens will probably range from f/1.2 or f/1.4 through to f/16 or f/22, so f/11 passes half the amount of light passed by f/8. The maximum aperture is marked on the front of a lens as, for example, 1:1.4/50. This last figure of 50 is the focal length of the lens in millimetres and indicates the angle of view (see Lenses).

Depth of field As you 'stop down' your lens, you narrow the beam of light passing through, and the image becomes progressively darker. Stopping down also creates a useful optical effect. It increases the zone of sharp focus, or *depth of field*, bringing more of the field of view into focus. Depth of field is also related to the angle of view of the lens. Wide-angle lenses have a generous depth of field, and practically the entire scene

Wire fencing (below) can be eliminated or reduced (but not cage bars) by moving in close, keeping a wide aperture and focusing on the subject.

Depth of field is much reduced in close-up shots, so you have to stop right down and use a slow shutter speed to increase the zone of sharp focus (above right and far right).

Subjects in shadow (right) or against the light may need wide apertures. Cameras with a backlight control will make exposure compensation (see Exposure), but depth of field may be shallow. Focus on subject's eyes if in doubt.

APERTURE AND DEPTH

is naturally in focus. Long, or 'tele', lenses have a shallow depth of field, so accurate focusing is more critical. By focusing on a subject and stopping down, the zone of sharpness extends both behind and in front of the point focused on. The degree, however, varies according to the camera-to-subject distance. At about 1m (3ft) from the camera, depth of field extends one third in front and two-thirds behind—the zone is always greater **behind** the subject than in front of it, unless you are very close, when the zone is equidistant. When do you need maximum depth of field? When you want everything sharply in focus, and this is often the case in still-life shots, landscapes and interiors. A useful technique in establishing maximum depth of field is to employ what is called the 'hyperfocal distance'—the nearest point that is acceptably sharp when your lens is focused on infinity. If you focus your lens on this point you will get maximum depth of field through the range of apertures. At f/16 or f/22 depth of field stretches from about 3m (10ft) to infinity.

The hyperfocal distance also depends on the lens focal length. With a 24mm wide-angle, the zone extends from under 1m (3ft) to infinity at f/16, while a 135mm lens gives only 13m (42ft) to infinity at the same f stop. If wide-angle lenses have such an extensive depth of field why not use them for close-up shots?

Depth of field varies according to the lens focal length. Wide-angle lenses have an inherently great depth of field, as shown in the shot of Le Mans (opposite), taken on a Pentax with a Takumar 35mm lens. **Extremely shallow** depth of field is a characteristic of long-focus lenses: the apple was shot with a Tamron 500mm mirror lens from a distance of about 9m (30ft). **Macro lenses** have such a shallow depth of field that fine-tune focusing is needed. The butterfly posed for a shot with a Vivitar 28–200mm zoom on the macro setting. Problems that arise with haze and areas of marked contrast (foreground versus background) can be tackled by stopping down (see bracketing p.61) The third picture (below) is a compromise of the first two shots.

APERTURE AND DEPTH

With a 28mm lens you can focus as close as 18cm (7in) but perspective is exaggerated and distorts the image.

Depth of field scales, as shown in the box below, are not found on many zoom lenses. The two-touch zoom, where there is one ring for focusing and another for zooming, doesn't provide scales since there isn't any room on the lens barrel.

An alternative is to use the depth of field preview, or stop down, button on your SLR, or the 'one-third, two-thirds' rule. This is a rule of optics that says depth of field extends one-third in front and two-thirds behind a subject in focus or a point of focus. It only begins to come into effect at f/4, and the zone increases as you stop down.

Depth of field preview is omitted on some cameras, mostly the autofocus SLRs, although Minolta's 9000AF has a preview button, and so have the Canon EOS 620 and 650 cameras. The unique EOS 650, as mentioned previously, has programmed depth of field, a facility that other manufacturers are bound to copy.

Using a zoom lens gives you plenty of scope to try various positions and angles of view. Zooming in on your subject, here a peregrine falcon, shows the combined effects of selective focusing and cropping. As the angle of view narrows the background goes out of focus, giving prominence to the subject.

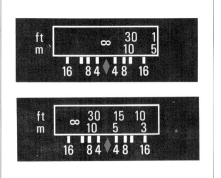

Depth of field scale on a lens gives two sets of numbers from f/4 to f/16. Top diagram tells you that at f/11, focus extends from 10m (30ft) to infinity. If you move the infinity mark ∞ to 16, everything is now sharp from 3m (10ft) to infinity.

SHUTTER
$\triangleright$ AND MOVEMENT $\triangleleft$

One of the functions of the shutter is to 'freeze' or register movement. When light has passed through the aperture it arrives at the shutter, which remains open for longer in weak light, or slams shut to protect the film in strong light. If your camera did not have a shutter you would have to control the light with a lens cap, as they did in the pioneering days of photography: with modern fast films your picture would be overexposed and movement would appear as a blur — not ideal in, say, a portrait. Blur is really a series of overlapping images as lightwaves register movement across the film, but blur can be effective to suggest action, as in the picture above.

SHUTTER AND MOVEMENT

The shutter decides the period of admission of light. Shutter and diaphragm work together at a ratio that is always constant, in steps that halve or double the exposure according to the setting. Thus, 1/500th at f/2.8 is the same exposure as ⅛th at f/22. The fast shutter would freeze movement and the wide aperture would allow selective focusing. The second ratio would blur movement but increase depth of field.

Compact camera shutters are mostly programmed and electromagnetic. They may be of the leaf-type set between the lens elements, or be behind the lens where the blades also serve as the aperture diaphragm. Since they are automatic, there's not much that you can do about controlling the speeds, which may range from as slow as 10 seconds (Olympus XA) to 1/500th seconds and up to 1/2000th second (Vivitar TW 35). If you want to blur the image, you may have to use slow film combined with a neutral density (ND) filter (see also

Compacts, p. 30). SLRs have focal plane shutters (invented by the English photographer William England in 1861); this type of shutter prevents light reaching the film when the lens is removed or when light passes through the lens in the reflex system. The shutter comprises two blinds, of cloth or metal, and both travel across the film plane in the same direction, either vertically or horizontally. The first blind moves across to expose the film, the second blind 'chases' the other at the pre-set speed. Thus, a variable-width slit is

created that scans and exposes the film, from 1 second to 1/1000th second or briefer (several SLRs can reach speeds of 1/4000th second). Obviously, a fast shutter speed gives such a brief exposure that you need to compensate with a wide aperture, unless the light is extremely bright, otherwise your picture would be under-exposed and dark.

The shutter of your camera can give you some wonderfully varied effects. With a fast shutter of 1/1000th second you can freeze a waterfall or a wave smashing against

1/30th sec

1/60th sec

1/125th sec

1/250th sec

1/500th sec

1/1000th sec

Speeding traffic can be slowed down by using progressively faster shutter speeds (above), set on the shutter dial (left). The picture at the top of the page was shot at 1/15th second—any slower and the cars would have disappeared. At 1/1000th second in the final shot, the car has been 'frozen'. Another means of stopping motion is to use electronic flash or, in scientific work, special shutters such as the Kerr cell, that attain speeds of above 1 millionth of a second!

The beach boys were shot using a Nikon FA, fitted with a Nikkor 500mm mirror lens on Agfachrome 100, at about 1/500th second at f/8. Very fast shutter speeds are not necessary if you are some distance away from the subject (unless using a long lens). The closer you get, the faster the shutter needs to be. In theory, you should be able to achieve this kind of action shot with a compact camera, since many attain speeds of 1/500th second in bright light. Then enlarge the main area of interest afterwards.

SHUTTER AND MOVEMENT

a rock. At 1/500th second you can stop a football in mid air or a sprinter running past. With fast-moving subjects, shutter speed is related to camera-to-subject distance and the direction of subject movement— either across your field of view of at an angle to the camera. The pictures on the previous pages show the relevant shutter speeds needed to blur or freeze passing traffic or racing cars (right). At a distance of 3m (9–10ft) a slow 1/15th second will blur a walker, while 1/250th second blurs a runner. At 2 seconds or more you can even blur a landscape (see pp. 132–3).

Freeze, pan and blur With a fast shutter of ¹⁄₁₀₀₀th second plus, you can stop a racing car dead as it passes by your stationary camera. **If you pan** with your lens, following the car through, and use a medium-fast speed, of, say, ¹⁄₅₀₀th second, the car stays sharp but the background blurs, giving an impression of speed and movements. See what happens when you pan at ¹⁄₁₂₅th second—everything becomes blurred. Best results are somewhere in between, like the shot on pages 148–9, where I used a shutter speed of ¹⁄₂₅₀th second.

▷ LENSES AND IMAGES ◁

Recent developments in camera lens design have done more to establish popular photography, generate enthusiasm and improve techniques of picture-taking than any other innovation. The variety of lenses available to SLR owners —especially zoom and autofocus lenses—has encouraged confidence and a greater freedom of pictorial expression. A manufacturer's survey found that the owners of zooms tended to favour the more extreme ranges of the lens, shooting either wide-angle or long-focus, no doubt in order to give pictures a fresh dimension by exploiting hitherto unusual angles of view. Interchangeable and zoom lenses also offer wider opportunities in terms of subject: landscape, architecture, sport and nature photography, for example, are categories that are well suited to the versatility and scope of variable focal lengths.

LENSES AND IMAGES

Camera lenses are a complex arrangement of optical glass elements—even a compact has a lens of 4 or more computer-designed elements, a zoom as many as 15. The function of each element is to improve resolution and reduce optical faults—aberrations—to a minimum. In addition to lenses made by major camera makers for their own cameras, there are many independent lens manufacturers whose products are of a high quality.

The photographer's main concern when choosing a lens is its maximum aperture and focal length, and these are related to each other. First, the focal length. This is the distance between the lens and film needed to form a sharp image when the lens is set at infinity. The field covered by the lens on the 35mm format is its angle of view. A standard lens has an angle of about 45°—equal to that of human vision. If you detach the standard lens from your camera, set it at infinity, and move the rear of the lens towards a piece of white card to form an image from, say, a nearby window, the image will come into focus 42mm from the rear of the lens. But strictly speaking, the measurement is taken from a point within the lens (the nodal point), and with most standard lenses this will be 50–55mm from the film plane. So your lens has a focal length of 50mm. Maximum aperture is found by dividing the focal length by the diameter of the iris diaphragm. This will be between 25mm and 30mm, giving an aperture of f/2 or f/1.8— the 'f' standing for 'focal length'. If you want to enlarge distant images, then you need a lens of longer focal length and narrower angle of view. Designers of long-focus lenses have managed to retain a short focal length, keeping the lens acceptably compact, while maintaining a large image. This is the 'telephoto' principle. The range of focal lengths from wide-angle lenses, with their very short focal lengths, through the standard to the long-focus lenses is shown below and opposite.

To sum up, wide angle lenses include more of a scene than a standard 50mm lens, but will exaggerate perspective—an effect that can be pictorially advantageous. A long focus lens acts like a telescope and magnifies distant objects, but foreshortens and flattens perspective.

15mm

24mm

28mm

35mm

50mm

135mm

200mm

300m

500mm

1000mm (500mm + 2 × converter)

15mm   24mm   28mm   35–70mm   80–200mm   500mm

LENSES AND IMAGES

A camera can form an image without the agency of a lens, as shown on page 41, but to produce an image free of faults requires a compound lens, corrected against such faults as image distortion, chromatic aberration and astigmatism. Correction relies on the precise arrangement of specifically-constructed elements of optical glass, the design of which takes many calculations and is today performed by computer. The 'best part' of a lens lies along its axis where lightwaves are least bent, or refracted, and travel in straight lines to the film plane. At wide apertures—even with good-quality lenses—there may be some lack of definition at the edges of the field, especially in close-up, as the picture opposite shows. Yet wide apertures are desirable when shooting in low light, and in the design of long lenses. With a long lens, the lightwaves have further to travel to reach the film; they become weaker, and the lens has to 'project' the image while maintaining acceptable quality, with good covering power, contrast and resolution.

A 300mm lens with an aperture of f/2.8 (the widest available) allows you to use fast shutter speeds with medium speed films, but can cost eight times the price of the camera. Most of us settle for a modest f/5.6 lens and use faster film to give the difference of two or three stops. Wide-angle lenses will give you a panoramic view of landscapes, or cover a generous area in confined spaces, but they are subject to some distortion. This distortion, and often dramatic effects of perspective (see pp. 158–9), gives the wide-angle lens its distinctive image 'style', like that of the long-focus lens with its shallow depth of field and flattened perspective (below).

Mirror or reflex lenses generally have a focal length of 500mm, a fixed aperture of f/8 and incorporate two mirrors which internally reflect the image. The arrangement shortens the focal length, allowing for a lighter and more compact design. Ring-shaped out of focus highlights are characteristic or mirror lenses.

Image distortion from a wide-angle is acceptable in restricted spaces (top, far left) but not cityscapes (far left). You may need the widest aperture of a **standard lens** in candlelight, or for selective focus (top, centre and left) but **close-up shots** may lose edge definition (opposite). The solution? Use a tripod and stop down. Big **telephotos** bring distant figures up close (top and middle) but beware of **camera shake**, even with a tripod (above).

LENSES AND IMAGES—ZOOM LENSES

The zoom lens is the most notable single achievement in lens design since the introduction of the interchangable lens system. Zooms are gradually replacing the range of prime, or 'one-function', lenses, though many photographers maintain that zoom lenses are not up to the optical standards of prime lenses. But amateur photographers have taken the zoom seriously and are encouraging progress in lens development. Zooms are becoming lighter, faster and smaller. Now photographers can glide from wide-angle to close-up with a single movement, given such lenses as Vivtar's 28mm to 200mm lens above. Until recently many non-professionals were limited to the relative confines of their 50mm standard lens, owing both to cost and the fact that many were unaware of the scope offered by different focal lengths and their unique angles of view. A problem with zoom lenses is their current size and weight and somewhat reduced apertures of f/3.5 and f/4. A heavy zoom that sweeps from a 28mm to 200m can produce camera shake, even in the

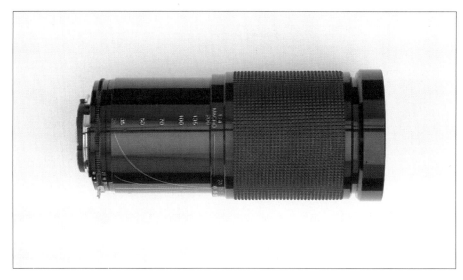

middle range. In bright Mediterranean sunlight, using ISO 100 film, to obtain maximum depth of field in a landscape at the 50mm setting, exposure gave 1/60th at f/16—fine on a standard lens, but you can't hand-hold a 200mm lens at speeds slower than 1/250th. The versatility of the superzoom is well acknowledged but you might be better off with a 28mm–70mm, and a 70mm–200mm. Most zooms include a macro setting, although they produce an image only about ¼ life size, while the true macro, such as Vivitar's 55mm f/2.8, gives an image of 1:1—this is not, however, a zoom lens. Zoom lenses can create images that have almost become photographic clichés, such as the shot below, made by pulling the zoom control ring back during an exposure of about 2 secs at f/11 on Fuji chrome ISO 50.

EXPOSURE
▷ AND LIGHT ◁

The combination of aperture and shutter determines the total amount of light allowed to reach the film. But we also have to take into account the film's speed—some films are more sensitive than others—related to the brightness of the subject, the nature of the subject, the direction of the light, and so on. The scene above was given a long exposure—2 seconds—with light-reducing filters and slow film, to record the effect of foliage in a high wind. Exposure is the single most critical aspect of photography, since the medium of photography is light in all its subtle shifts of intensity, colour and mood. This is why designers of SLRs are continually improving their exposure metering systems.

EXPOSURE AND LIGHT

Most cameras have a built-in meter. SLRs have a through-the-lens (TTL) system; compacts have automatic programming for both shutter and aperture. So have some SLRs, and in addition provision for manual operation, or aperture- and shutter-priority programmes (Ap and Sp). Can't go wrong? Well, you can, which is why seasoned photographers use a hand-held meter to confirm a doubtful exposure.

Exposure is the result of a selected balance between aperture and shutter, according to the photographer's requirements and the nature of the subject. Fast shutter? Then you'll need a wider aperture. Stop down for depth of field? You will have to select a slower shutter speed.

Exposure is the 'make or break' of picture-taking. Too much light and your picture is washed out, with bleached colours and no vigour, while black and white negatives appear thin and ghostly. Too little light and the picture is gloomy and sombre with dark shadows.

Compact cameras and automatic SLRs work out the correct exposure for us, though what is 'correct' may be debatable and subjective; over-exposure can produce attractive, high-key shots, and underexposure will intensify colours. Cameras with integral TTL (through-the-lens) meters can 'spot' read from a small, selected area, others are centre-weighted, or 'subject-weighted', to read from a central area, others take separate light readings from various parts of the scene to give a computed result.

Camera through-the-lens (TTL) metering (above) may take spot readings from a small area, while **centre-weighted** has a bias towards the centre of the scene, and **overall** generalises brightness over entire area of view.

House and garden shots show results of different readings. 1. **Spot reading** for dark shadows alone overexposes rest of scene. 2. **General foreground** reading gives better tonal balance, but is still overexposed. 3. **Centre-weighted** reading gives acceptable exposure but shadows lose detail. 4. **Highlight reading** darkens shadows and sky.

At al fresco lunch, midday (right), readings were taken of the food display, then the shot was slightly underexposed to enrich colour and detail. This caused surrounding shadows to darken, and emphasised the main point of interest.

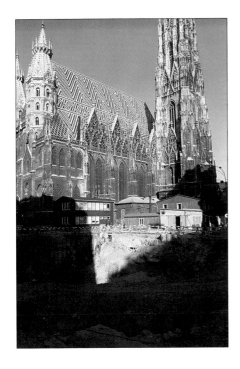

TTL meter (above) cannot cope with extreme contrast, reading for light areas only.
Exposing for highlights (centre) creates atmosphere, absent in the balanced exposure (right). **Exposing for shadows** overexposes the beach (far right), producing sunnier aspect than the 'correct' exposure (right).
Overexposed winter scene (below) gives a high-key effect. **Underexposed summer shade** (right) is low key and atmospheric.

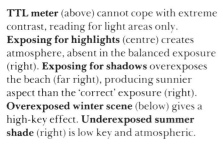

EXPOSURE AND LIGHT

There was a time when problems of exposure became an obsession with photographers and some may even be sorry to lose this preoccupation. What most of us want in a picture is a good representative spread of colour hues and tonal values, from highlights to dark areas, yet with a degree of punchy contrast. We want the photograph to represent the subject as seen by the eye, and we don't really wish to go into lengthy calculations in order to achieve this. We can leave that to the camera.

Sophisticated metering systems, such as Nikon's FA camera, the Canon T90, the Olympus OM4 and others, can read light bouncing off water, peer into the darkest shadows, assess the medium tones of farm buildings, handle the contrast of bright blue sky on one side of the scene, and storm clouds brewing on the other, and give you an exposure of, say, 1/125th second at f/12.5 that will cover the lot!

Even a modest compact can tackle backlit subjects, and budget priced SLRs will give accurate exposure reading, nine times out of ten. Yet there are photographers —myself included—who still pack a hand-held meter, such as the Weston Master or one of those shown here, on the right. Why? Because they are useful to those who work with slide film where exposure latitudes are narrow, and can make all the difference between a successful picture and one you wish you'd got right. They work in low light, and when shooting doubtful subjects of very high key, or extremes of contrast when it helps to take readings from highlights and shadows. Also they are valuable for taking incident light readings.

Incident readings measure light falling on the subject as distinct from reflected light, a useful means of exposing for distant subjects. The

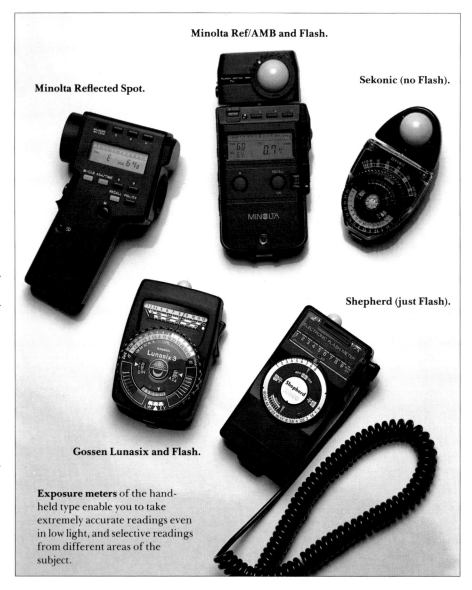

Minolta Ref/AMB and Flash.

Minolta Reflected Spot.

Sekonic (no Flash).

Shepherd (just Flash).

Gossen Lunasix and Flash.

Exposure meters of the hand-held type enable you to take extremely accurate readings even in low light, and selective readings from different areas of the subject.

opaque domed diffuser on a meter, or the Invercone attachment on the Weston meter, is not adversely influenced by highlights and subject brightness. To take an incident reading, point your meter diffuser at the camera.

Backlight TTL readings (below) can fool the camera's meter because the lens is pointing towards strong light, and the meter's reaction is to stop down. This ignores the shadow areas, which remain underexposed. A reading pointing at the light bouncing off the lawn gave ¹⁄₂₅₀th second at f/11 (right). A reading for the shadows alone gave ¹⁄₂₅₀th second at f/3.5, which would have overexposed the rest of the scene. An overall reading recommended ¹⁄₂₅₀th second at f/5.6 (left) and the centre shot is a compromise— ¹⁄₂₅₀th second at f/8.

Snow scenes, and subjects dominated by dazzling highlights, such as sun on water, require more selective metering. You can 'bracket' doubtful subjects (see right) or use the duplex method, where you take two incident readings, one from the camera, another from the light source, and then average both readings.

Some hand-held meters give accurate spot readings of narrow, selected areas, even of subjects some distance away. Most meters will also take readings for electronic flash and they are invaluable for studio lighting. A TTL meter has some of the advantages of a hand-held meter, and it can be similarly employed. You can, for instance, fit a diffuser to your standard lens for incident light readings. Another way of using your TTL meter is to point the lens at various parts of the scene and note the responses of the meter. This will give you a good idea of extremes of light levels, and see the subject much as the camera sees it. Even an 'average' scene will give you half a dozen separate exposure readings.

Figure in shadow (left) poses fewer exposure problems than one in direct sunlight. A hand-held meter allows you to take a selective reading from the shadows alone. For the **figure (right)** you would need to take readings for both the shadows and highlights, and choose a setting in between, or take an incident light reading.

1/125 second at f/8

1/125 second at f/11

1/125 second at 12.5

1/125 second at f/16

Bracketing is a 'fail safe' way of making sure you get an acceptable exposure, especially with slide film, and gives you a choice from a range of exposures. The technique is to shoot the subject at the recommended TTL exposure, then at one or two f stops either side. The meter's 'correct' exposure for the cottage above, for example, was 1/125th second at f/12.5. In fact, f/11 is perhaps more acceptable, with whiter snow. At f/16 the result is too dark. If you use a zoom lens and change the focal length while bracketing, as in the first two shots above, you will get different readings—a long-focus shot needs longer exposure than a wide-angle, so keep the same angle of view throughout.

Some cameras have a provision for automatic bracketing. The Canon EOS 620AF has this facility, so does the Contax 167MT (above) which brackets two full stops in either direction.

EXPOSURE AND LIGHT

Two professional methods of obtaining average readings are the grey card technique and reading from the back of your hand (as a grey card substitute). The photographic industry has adopted a standard scale of reflectance that best approximates average monochrome tones of everyday subjects. This has been arrived at as 18 per cent grey, and cameras, film and meters are gauged accordingly.

To take a grey card reading, place the card in incident light and take a reading from the surface, but be careful that your camera doesn't throw shadows on the card. A grey card would give you an average for any of the scenes below, except for the interior shot. For this I had to measure the outside scene, take another for the highlights on the table, and one of the foreground. Readings ran from f/11 to f/3.5. I bracketed around f/6.3, which turned out to be the best exposure.

Any exposure may need to take into account the atmosphere or mood that a scene evokes, and this is another instance where bracketing is valuable, since it might be the difference of only a half to a whole stop either way. A TTL meter takes account of any filters on the lens, but if you use a hand-held meter you'll have to add the filter factor to your calculations, since most filters absorb some light. An exposure increase of one-third of a stop is average, though some filters have factors of two or three stops or more.

Castle at Vaduz, Liechtenstein (above and above right) taken at the camera's recommended TTL (centre-weighted) reading of ¹/₁₂₅th second at f/8, on Agfachrome ISO 100 film. At least two stops underexposure was needed to register the background and to create mood and atmosphere in the scene. To enrich the colour of this **seascape at Brighton** (right), I underexposed by about 1–1½ stops, intensifying the sea and sky (below).

Lakeland and garden (opposite) are a feature of this restaurant in the Hambledon Hall hotel, Rutland. **The long shot**, below, recorded tables, but the windows are 'burned out'. The solution was to move nearer to the window, and stop down, using a slower shutter speed with Kodak Ektachrome 200 film and a 35mm wide-angle lens.

EXPOSURE AND LIGHT

Errors that might have been avoided:
Bluebells (right) taken on Fujichrome 100
film. Flowers were in shadow and the
foreground exposure read ¹⁄₁₅th second at
f/3.5. I was without a tripod so I supported my
Nikon FA on a stick, and held my breath.
Even so, the result shows camera shake. **Flare
spots** (below) were caused by shooting into the
light without a lens hood. **Subject movement**
(bottom, left), results from using slowish film
(ISO 64) at ¹⁄₆₀th second and the widest
aperture of f/3.5. With no tripod, a slower
shutter would have meant camera shake; a
faster shutter, underexposure. **Blue film
crew** at dusk (below right) shot on a long
exposure because I had neglected to bring
flash equipment. Exposure was ¹⁄₈th second at
f/3.5 on Ektachrome 400 film.

FILM
▷ AND PROCESSES ◁

A film emulsion—the coating of light-sensitive silver compounds that forms the image, invisible, or 'latent', until it has been developed in the darkroom—is capable of recording infinite variations of tone, from bright light to deep shadow. The structure of the emulsion varies according to the degree of sensitivity, or 'speed'. Highly sensitive 'fast' films can be used in weak light, or when you need to use a fast shutter for action pictures. Slow films are chosen to record fine detail and to give crisp definition and faithful colour rendering. Fast films have a grainy, textured appearance when the image is enlarged—the faster the film, the more pronounced the grain. New technology, though, is producing fast films with a minimum of grain, notably the 'T-grain' (tablet grain) emulsions pioneered by Kodak and adopted by Agfa and Fuji.

FILM AND PROCESSES

35mm film is contained inside a metal cassette, in lengths producing 12, 24 or 36 pictures. Colour print film is by far the most popular, with slide film and black and white film trailing way behind. Films are rated according to the sensitivity of their emulsion. ISO 25 is a slow, fine-grained film, ISO 400 is fast, ISO 1600, ultra-fast—and grainy. Many photographers choose the happy medium of ISO 100 for general-purpose photography. Most popular films are DX coded, which automatically registers on the camera's film-speed setting.

There are two kinds of photographic film—a negative (either black and white or colour) from which you obtain a positive print; and a slide or positive transparency. Slide film is almost invariably in colour, although one film manufacturer, Agfa, makes a black and white positive slide film called Dia-Direct.

Colour print film is the choice of over 90 percent of camera owners, and its main appeal is that results can be easily displayed in an album, stored for ready reference or distributed among friends or as examples of your work. You can also have prints enlarged and display them in frames. It is possible to obtain prints from transparencies, as in the Cibachrome process, but this is more expensive than prints from negatives, although results can be excellent.

The international film speed ratings, ISO (International Standards Organization), have replaced the standard ASA (American Standards Association) but the numbering remains the same, but this hardly affects owners of DX-recognition cameras. However, there can be drawbacks to DX coding if your camera is a compact where coded film-speed settings cannot be overridden.

For example there may be occasions when it is useful to change the speed setting because some films are improved by slight under- or overexposure. Print film, for example, can be improved by marginal overexposure, especially in conditions of bright sunlight, and with the high contrast and blue sky associated with the Mediterranean.

Where a camera underexposes to compensate for bright light (the aperture stops down to avoid **overexposure**, thus losing the medium tones and shadow detail) your prints may turn out dull and flat, but by setting the camera's ISO dial to ISO 100, when using ISO 200 film, you effectively overexpose by one stop—speed ratings proceed in steps of one stop, ISO 50; ISO 64; ISO 100; ISO 200, and so on.

Compact cameras automatically set a speed of ISO 100 with **non-DX-coded film**. By putting ISO 200 print film in your camera, and covering the coding squares on the cassette with insulating tape, you can cheat the system.

Changing a film speed rating is known as 'pushing', or uprating. It is useful when, for example, you are shooting in weak light and you need a faster shutter speed. What you do is rate the film higher, so that 1/30th second at f/2 using ISO 100 would give you a more managable 1/125 at f/2 if you pushed the film two stops to ISO 400.

An uprated film has to be push-processed, or overdeveloped. This has the effect of increasing grain and contrast. There will be a loss of colour or colour casts will occur and the technique is only really suitable with slide film or black and white. If you process your own black and white white film, give a 40 percent increase of development for every stop pushed.

The huge market for colour print film does not quite match the choice available. There are more types of colour slide, or transparency, film (also known as 'reversal' film because, during processing, it reverses from a negative to a positive image).

Slide films allow little room for correction, unlike prints, so a photographer has to decide on the quality and colour rendition of a particular make of film. It may be a matter of taste, detail or permanence. Kodachrome 64, for example, is the choice of many professionals because of its sure colour quality, fine grain and archival permanence (it will not fade over a period of years).

Broadly speaking, Fuji films have a bias towards yellow and red; Agfa films are generally warm in tone, while Kodak films are cooler, especially Ektachrome with its slight blue

Your choice of film depends on the subject, location and expected light conditions. **Slow speed films** have fine 'grain' but are less sensitive than fast films: the faster the film, the coarser the grain, although recent developments are producing fast, finer-grain films. You need **slow films** (ISO 25 or 50) for bright light, such as this shot in California at high noon, or to register fine detail and delicate colour, as in the bouquet of flowers (opposite). **Medium speed** (ISO 100) films are a good choice for 'everyday' subjects—family picnics, good colour detail; medium fast (ISO 200–400) are useful for action shots, and for interiors illuminated by available light (above). **Fast** (ISO 400) to **ultrafast** (ISO 1000 and 1600) for sports shots with long-focus lenses, or for deliberate grain effects in, for example, glamour and fashion photography. The shot (right) was made on Fuji 1600 slide film, and enlarged.

FILM AND PROCESSES

bias. Colour print films have a wider degree of latitude, or tolerance to variations of exposure, and many inaccuracies can be corrected at the printing stage. But with colour slides you are on your own.

Slide film is more sensitive to slight variations in exposure and you have to be accurate if you are to obtain acceptable results. Slide film images are sharper than those of a print, with a more subtle and wider tonal range and contrast.

Because prints undergo an extra stage in processing—that of conversion from the negative to the positive image—and because the paper absorbs some of the colour, there is bound to be a slight loss of definition and saturation compared with that of a slide.

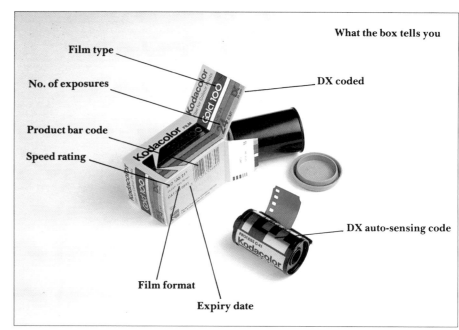

What the box tells you

Film type
No. of exposures
Product bar code
Speed rating
DX coded
DX auto-sensing code
Film format
Expiry date

Snooker table shot on Agfachrome (left), Ektachrome (centre) and Fujichrome (right), all ISO 100 film, all identical exposures with studio electronic flash. Only very slight differences are apparent. **The girl** (below) was shot of Fujichrome 100 (left) and Ektachrome 100 (right) by daylight, and colour differences are more apparent. **The fanlight** (far right) and **chefs** (opposite) were shot on ultra-fast Fuji 1600 and Kodacolor 1000 respectively, and show good colour accuracy, saturation and, considering the grain, detail.

Filters for colour Where films are balanced to a particular colour 'temperature' a filter may be unnecessary. But shoot daylight film by tungsten (see p. 70) and you will need to correct the balance with a **blue filter 80A**. Tungsten film in daylight needs a **pale orange 85B filter**. Use an **81A** for 'warming up' skin tones on daylight film, and a **polariser** for enriching colour. The all-purpose **skylight** filter has a slightly warming effect.

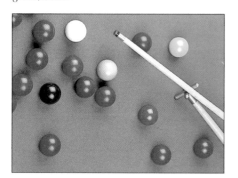

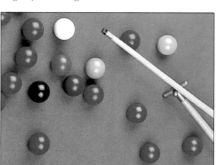

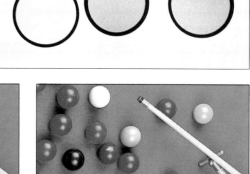

You can have fun with infrared or 'IR' film, in black and white and in colour, but there are snags with the processing of colour film. For one thing, IR colour is developed by the E4 process, whereas colour laboratories are geared to the E6 slide film process. E4 has to be developed by hand, so it is worthwhile doing your own developing if you intend to regularly use IR colour film. Black and white IR can be developed by normal processing techniques. There are two types: Kodak's High Speed Infrared, rated at ISO 80 for daylight, and ISO 200 in tungsten; Kodak Ektachrome IR colour film, rated at ISO 100 in daylight, and ISO 50 in tungsten. As infrared radiation is outside the visible spectrum you cannot see infrared effects, and you have to experiment with films and filters: the infrared content in dull weather, for example, is much lower than on a fine day. Filters to use are Wratten 12 with colour, and 25 or 29 red with black and white. Dramatic colour effects can be achieved by using IR with a variety of filters.

Dull weather reduces IR radiation and makes for slow speeds—(right). These pictures were taken early on Christmas morning at the Serpentine Swimming Club, where members have taken the plunge each Christmas since the mid 19th century. The top picture was shot minus a filter and shows the cast characteristic of infrared.

FILM AND PROCESSES

Print film is usually returned to the photographer in the form of machine-processed enprints which can sometimes be disappointing. Yet, to be fair, enprints are only a guide to the end result, although most find their way into albums. They do not really show the potential of the original negative, or the print quality that can be achieved by a good colour laboratory.

The majority of slide films are process-paid (purchase of the film includes processing and mounting of slides) and the service may depend on the type of film. Koda-chrome, for example, has to be sent away for processing by a unique process known as K-14, where colour dyes are added during de-

An **underexposed negative** produces a dark print (left) but correction shows flat colour, loss of contrast and a milky cast (below).
Overexposed negative (far left) yields a better result when corrected (below). Filtration during printing can restore colour and, to a certain extent, eliminate casts. The rule is—overexpose print film, underexpose slide film, since print film has a greater latitude, or tolerance. The family scene was shot on Kodacolor Gold 100.

velopment.

Kodak Ektachrome, on the other hand, is a triple-decker film, a 'sandwich' of layers of emulsion and dye molecules. If you are in a hurry to see your pictures you can buy non-process-paid Ektachrome because it can be developed by independent laboratories using the E6 process.

Where processing is carried out by the film's manufacturers, packing is provided with the film to be returned in, and results may take a week or more according to the season—obviously, there's a heavy demand on the laboratories after the summer holidays.

Professional films are mostly non-process paid. There isn't a great deal of difference, however, between professional film and the amateur product. Professional film leaves the factory in peak condition for optimum performance, and needs to be kept refrigerated. A further advantage is that they can be purchased in bulk, in reference to a batch number that ensures precise colour rendition over a number of rolls of film and, as the photographer may be in a hurry, they can all be developed by the fast E6 process.

Mountaineer Chris Bonington in Cumbria shot on Ektachrome 100 slide film. Copying a transparency to correct under- or overexposure may alter colour and increase contrast. Underexposed slide (far left) allows only marginal correction (left) and is hardly worthwhile. Underexposed slide (bottom, left) can be lightened (below) with loss of colour. The rule is—try and be spot on with slide film exposures, but always err towards underexposure rather than overexposure.

FILM AND PROCESSES

Slide film emulsions are balanced either for daylight (type A) or for tungsten (type B). Tungsten is artificial light and includes domestic lighting, street lamps and photolamps. Daylight film can be used with flash and fluorescent tubes. Print film is suitable for all lighting conditions, since prints are colour corrected at the printing stage.

Colour slide film is sensitive to colour casts, effects of light not visible to the eye, seen by the camera, and they may have a marked effect on the film. Casts can add atmosphere to your picture and are not necessarily undesirable, but some may have an adverse effect—a

portrait under foliage may have a greenish glow that you will have to filter out—an 81A, or a magenta filter will absorb green light.

Blue casts are prominent in the early morning, in snow scenes or misty landscapes. Orange and red casts can appear in morning and evening light. The same effect will occur if you shoot pictures with daylight film in domestic light. This can be attractive, giving the shot a warm glow, but the colour can be filtered out in printing, or by the addition of a blue 80A filter to the front of your lens when shooting.

Modern films are wonderfully versatile. All have their special

characteristics and their individual response to the effects of light. There is a film to suit every subject, and it is well worth experimenting with the ever-increasing range of types from the different manufacturers. Photographers may argue —and do constantly—that such and such a film is better than another, but in the end it all depends on individual style, approach and, of course, the subject itself. I have stated where appropriate the films used to shoot many of the pictures in this book, so that you can compare and judge the result for yourselves.

Colour casts:
Daylight shot on **tungsten film**, no filter (top); **daylight film** by tungsten, no filter (above); **daylight film** in floodlamp, no filter (above right). Green cast in mid-morning on **Ektachrome film** (right), and by light filtering through foliage (far right), both without filters. Casts can, in fact, be effective and colour correction filters are not always necessary.

72

Natural colour casts can occur at any time of the day; late evening (above), early morning light (above centre) and midday (above right). The strong orange cast was recorded at sunset, in Cyprus. Atmospheric effects play a large part, so blue casts will occur where there is haze, mist or spray. This is because tiny water droplets reflect and scatter the short (blue) wavelengths of light; the blueness of distant hills is due to this phenomenon.

Reciprocity failure. The inability of a film emulsion to render colour accuratly during long or very short ($\frac{1}{2000}$th second) exposures. It is a rather rare condition. My dictionary says: "the principle according to which the density of the image formed when an emulsion is developed is directly proportional to the duration of the exposure and the intensity of the light." The principle ceases to be valid with abnormal exposures. In other words, the film cannot cope and false colours are registered, usually violet. The shot of **Coniston, Cumbria** (above) was at 9 a.m. on a misty morning. At dusk (right) a longer exposure was needed, about 2 secs, and the violet cast is beginning to appear.

Photographer Adrian Flowers, shot in the mid 1950s when by mutual agreement all film manufacturers altered their film speeds overnight. This was because processing machinery recently introduced was unable to cope with the density of black and white emulsion; the way to produce a thinner negative was to change the film speed, uprating it by a stop. Thus Ilford's FP3 at ASA 200 became ASA 400. This picture was taken on Ilford HPS, ASA 400. The speed rating ASA is now known as ISO.

3

► BLACK ◄
AND WHITE

BLACK AND WHITE

Black and white has a simple, direct quality which we accept just as readily as a colour picture, judging it in its own right and not as a substitute for colour. Our attitude to black and white photography is due to our having made a convention of the black and white image, partly out of necessity, but mainly in recognition of its exceptional characteristics.

Until the 1960s, when colour film became thoroughly established, there was no practical alternative, black and white had been the norm since Niépce produced the world's first photograph in 1827. Out of that state of affairs there grew a tradition where photography gradually formed its own definitive, pictorial principles and conventions.

Formal, purist even, the black and white picture has a sort of monumental quality and a more intrinsic structure than a comparable colour shot. In a colour picture, the colour itself can be the subject—a red poppy, a blue door, a green umbrella. Remove the colour and the eye needs some substance of interest—a finely dispersed range of tones, a balance of black and white masses, a vigorous juxtaposition of contrast and so on.

Black and white offers a strength and simplicity that more easily conveys mood and atmosphere; it can sustain greater drama and impact—and, in photoreportage and sport, a starkness that readily displays urgency—the right stuff of news. Yet it is a medium that can also be gentle, ethereal and romantic, the first requirement of many landscape and portrait photographers.

Working with black and white film stimulates a serious approach to photography, since it is inseparable from the darkroom where you continue the image-making process under the enlarger. For many, this is 'the best part' of photography, the most rewarding and engrossing, where the negative is only the beginning. A print can transform the basic image contained in the negative and, to the keen photographer, every negative is a rich source of inspiration.

Black and white film has a wonderful quality of recording the dispersion of subtle tones, balance of contrast and the rendering of strong, simple shapes, especially in portraits. **Playwright and actor Alan Bennett** (below left) and **cartoonist Mel Calman**, (right), photographed in daylight on Ilford FP4 with a Canon T90 camera.

The Lindsay brothers (below right) attempt a formal pose. The film was probably FP3 rated at ASA 64. Camera unremembered.

BLACK AND WHITE

Go and look for black and white subjects. Ask yourself, 'would this be better in black and white rather than in colour?' Interpreting subjects in black and white, bearing in mind that the medium presents subject matter minus the frills of colour, can be less compromising but needs careful attention to composition and lighting.

People often refer to the 'abstract' quality of black and white pictures because monochrome accentuates shape and pattern, and light areas are more sharply delineated than in colour, standing out against dark areas. Also, we see the world about us in colour, so black and white images are 'abstract'. Photographers working in black and white are care-ful with the arrangement of shapes and the balancing of mass against detail, in which respect films offer a wide scope.

Black and white film has a famously generous exposure latitude, where you could probably make errors of two or more stops either way, and still get acceptable results. Films range from Kodak's Technical Pan, rated at ISO 25, to Kodak Recording film rated at ISO 1000. Technical Pan will give you exceptionally fine grain, but needs to be processed in low-contrast Technidol developer.

Conventional films include Kodak's T-Max 100 and 400, employing the T-grain 'architecture' that gives speed with less grain.

Music centre, the Royal Albert Hall, taken on Kodak Tri-X film. A red No 25 filter, held over the lens of a Canon Sureshot compact, has darkened the sky, but washed out the red brickwork. Although a contrasty subject, shadow detail is good.

Quartet rehearsal, Holland 1950's displaying flare from a sunlit window. This gives the shot a soft, atmospheric quality so nicely captured by fast black and white film. Dated it certainly is; the lens may have been of the pre-anti-halation type designed to subdue flare; the film is Ilford HPS 400; and the camera probably an Exacta.

Quartet rehearsal, London, 1987 using flash and Ilford XPl film which registers fine detail. Any loss of atmosphere is made up for by the quartet's personal appeal and sense of fun—Mozart included. Camera used was a Canon T90 with 300TL speedlight.

The Serpentine Swimming Club,
Christmas morning. Canon Sureshot
camera, Ektachrome 100 film.

THE SELECTIVE EYE

THE SELECTIVE EYE — TAKING PICTURES

A successful photograph reflects the photographer's judgement and confirms his skill to himself and the viewer of the picture. Having spotted the potential in a subject, and rapidly assessed all the factors involved—camera position, angle of view, exposure—he has snatched the moment in time and recorded it for his own personal pleasure.

A photograph may also reflect much advanced planning and preparation. Having decided on a likely source of material, the photographer has anticipated the moment and place where the most promising shots will occur and has put himself in the right place at the right time.

Time is usually on the photographer's side. One enthusiast said that he had waited **three years** for the right conditions of light to strike a particular landscape and, in the end, had been well rewarded. In photography, as in all things in life, there is the element of chance—the element that has been responsible for some of photography's greatest pictures.

Obviously, some subjects make better pictures than others. Some photographs rely entirely on the strength of the subject, and very little on interpretation, but for the most part the photographer needs to influence or manipulate the subject in some way,

perhaps by the arrangement of the setting or surroundings, by an unusual angle of view or the unusual quality of the light.

Light itself can be the subject of a picture. The two shots on this page depend almost entirely on the effects of light on landscape. In one, the softening effects of early morning mist, in the other, a passing summer storm.

The main thing to aim for is simplicity. Make the subject dominant, or at least make the viewer aware of its influence. When appropriate, fill your viewfinder and be selective in composing the picture, eliminating extraneous detail unless, of course, that detail has something to add to the general effect.

Summer storm, Studland Bay, Dorset (opposite). I saw this storm building up and sprinted about half a mile to fetch my camera from the beach hut, and made it just in time. It's the contrast created by the white sails that makes the picture. Taken on a Nikon FA, 50mm standard lens and Ektachrome 100 film.

Buttermere in the Lake District, early morning (below). Slight mist combined with slight underexposure—about half a stop— has given the scene a delicate softness. Good depth of field from a 35mm wide-angle lens, and a nice balance of tones from Ektachrome 100 film. Taken on an Olympus OM2 SLR.

TAKING PICTURES

I have chosen the pictures in this section only to show that simple, everyday scenes have something to recommend them pictorially if you are selective. Some have relied on light, or on silhouette. Others on a gust of wind, a splash of colour, reflections in glass and in water, an arrangement of figures and shapes, the symmetry and harmony offered by composition according to the camera angle and the lens—things, in fact, that caught my eye.

The rugby football players, overleaf, were shot hurriedly, one frame after another. Choosing the best of the bunch came later, when I was able to select the most suitable shot from a sheet of contacts, the one that has the best range of expressions combined with peak action and a nice balance of shapes.

Look around you. Everything is photographable, but will anything make a picture? The arrangement of domestic objects to make a still life, perhaps, illuminated by daylight and shot with the lens closed down (for maximum depth of field) and the camera on a tripod; or a close-up shot with the macro setting of your zoom lens, studying the texture of fabric; or the range of colours in a box of crayons, an abstract pattern pleasing to the eye.

Frost on a window, or a crop of weeds sprouting from a cracked wall? A view against the light—or with the light behind you or perhaps with flash. Long focus lens—or wide angle lens? To filter or not to filter? The potential and rewards are endless. That's photography.

Things that catch the eye: the palace in **Delhi** framed by an arch; **Little Moreton Hall, Cheshire**, reflected in the moat; the **windmill** in the window, Kent; the guests at a **wedding**; the wind catching 1,500 empty **deckchairs, Hampstead**; a pile of **pumpkins, Boston, Mass**; a bouquet of **rainbow boots, Camden Town**. Keep an open mind, and a camera in your pocket.

TAKING PICTURES

What's in the picture? A pleasing arrangement of shapes, a spontaneous moment of humour—whatever beguiles the eye may make a worthwhile shot. On the other hand it may not . . . I liked the harmony of shapes (and the cat) in this conversation piece; the bull on the hill in Spain, the bather (shot with a compact clamped to binoculars); the wind-shaped tree and St. Michael's Mount; the curve of the railings in Bath.

Choice may also be made after the event. There are a number of possibles in this sheet of contact prints. I chose the picture that seemed to have the most tense action and symmetry. Taken on a Nikon F-501 autofocus SLR with a 70–210mm AF zoom.

ILFORD XP1 400 SAFETY FILM ILFORD

32 32A 33 33A 34 34A 35

ILFORD XP1 4CO SAFETY FILM ILFORD

14 14A 15 15A 16 16A 17

ILFORD XP1 400 SAFETY FILM ILFORD

20 20A 21 21A 22 22A 23

LIGHTING

The powerful, controlled lighting of a studio will give you a quite different type of picture than any achieved by natural light. Studio lighting even alters the **style** of the picture towards the type more associated with fashion magazines—the almost shadowless effects and flawless clarity set against a whiter than white background.

Studio lighting is the big brother of the flashgun, cool, fast and efficient. Since many cameras are equipped with either built-in flash or have facilities for flash dedication, the general effects and basic understanding of flash techniques and flash lighting are familiar to most enthusiasts; the techniques and applications of studio lighting are quite similar.

Studio flash gives a cool light approximating in colour temperature to daylight, and is extremely versatile in respect of power output and quality of light itself, ranging from a soft and delicate diffused illumination, to a harsh and brilliant high-key.

Non-professional but by no means unprofessional computer flash home studio kits, such as the Courtney system used here, give plenty of light if you gauge it correctly. Direct diffused flash can give you a nice high-key result, below, or soft and delicate modelling when bounced off an umbrella (right).

LIGHTING

Studio lighting arrangements usually comprise one or two flash heads with connecting cables and sync leads. A flash head carries a flash tube, and a modelling bulb that gives you a lighting preview, allowing you to judge the eventual effect the flash will have on your portrait. The modelling lamp can remain on through the session and is not powerful enough to affect exposure.

Each flash head has a channel to accept a 'brolly' reflector for bouncing the light—or you can fit barn doors to narrow the beam, a snoot to highlight hair, or a softbox diffuser to soften the light. The set-up used here was a Courtenay computer flash unit, which gives automatic exposure control similar to that used in some flashguns. The system has a remote sensor that fits on to the camera's hot shoe. All you need do is calculate the subject-to-flash distance and set the aperture on the sensor—there's a choice of f/5.6; f/8; f/11 at ISO 100, and also a manual setting. The sensor measures the light reflected by the subject and quenches flash output when the subject has received sufficient exposure. At ten feet from flash to subject, you can use either of the three aperture settings—f/11 for depth of field, for example, and the sensor gives the correct exposure. With computer flash you can use several heads automatically controlled by the one sensor.

Portrait (top right) taken with bounced flash, two reflectors, and a diffuser over the lens for a short-focus effect. Dark cloth background, Ektachrome 100 film. The shots below used a snoot to highlight the hair, bounced flash, almost frontal and high up, and a single reflector.

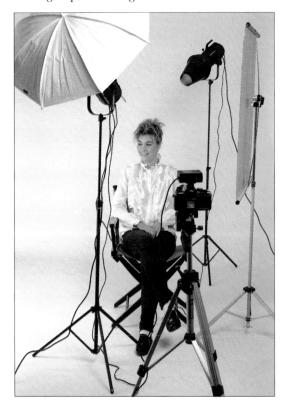

Two umbrellas and a reflector were needed to light the portrait (top right). I used a 500mm Nikkor mirror lens for the big close-up. **The effects** of positioning lighting is shown here, using a family group. Raking sidelight will create shadows on faces and on the wall. Best results were achieved by moving the group away from the wall, and using direct, diffused flash.

LIGHTING

Reflectors play an important role in lighting techniques, for glamour and fashion shots as well as for portraits. Even with a piece of white card, a compact camera, and sunlight streaming through a window (right), you can give detail to otherwise dark shadows. Reflectors were used in the pictures below and opposite, taken with professional studio flash, a professional model, and larger film format— 6cm × 6cm (2¼in × 2¼in). While professional studio flash is undeniably powerful, you can use the same techniques with amateur studio equipment to achieve pictures that compare favourably with the 'real thing.'

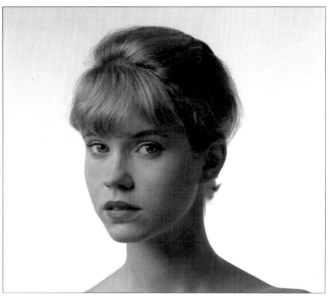

Single flash, softened by a 'soft box' studio diffuser to the left of the camera.

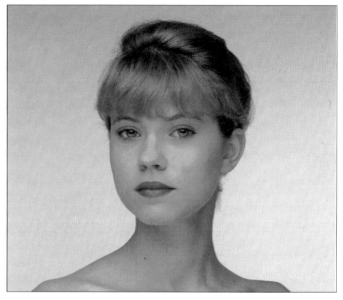

Same arrangement, but with a reflector to the right of the camera close to model's face.

Flash bounced off the background gave enough light to illuminate the model's face with reflectors placed in front.

Direct flash behind model's head lit two reflectors either side of the camera.

Soft box placed just to the camera's left
and a reflector to the right.

LIGHTING

There are occasions when flash is valuable and there is really no alternative form of lighting, especially in interiors with poor ambient light. The power and effect of flash depends on the subject distance and the aperture set on the camera. Shutter speed is synchronised to the flash at usually 1/125th second, or slower, the Olympus F280 is synchronised to speeds up to 1/1000th, the Canon 620 at 1/250th second.

Manual guns have a guide number (GN), and to gauge exposure you divide the GN for your film (usually ISO 100) by the subject distance to obtain the aperture, or a film speed/aperture/subject distance scale is provided, as on the press-type Metz gun (opposite page).

The majority of guns are automatic, with manual override, and they work by measuring the light reflected by the subject while the flash is actually firing. This is achieved by a control device called a thyristor, which calculates the exposure needed and economises power by quenching the light when exposure has been reached.

Recycling time depends on the size of the gun's capacitor, or power unit, and the subject distance: if the subject has needed a lot of light—bouncing light (below) means flash has a greater distance to travel—the recycling time is longer. Don't be impatient, though. It is a good idea to wait ten seconds after the flash-ready light has come on, in order to let the flash reach its re-charge peak.

Fast films, by the way, do not increase the power of the flash, but less light is needed to illuminate the subject. A gun's light is at its most powerful when directed at the subject, but the effect may be harsh with strongly cast shadows.

Flash heads are adjustable to enable you to alter the direction of the flash beam, and also have adjustments to widen or narrow the angle of the beam to suit the focal length of your lens. With a flash fitted to the hot shoe of your camera, you can select the position for either direct flash (diagram below, continuous lines) or bounced flash (dotted lines). Direct flash gives a strong frontal light and casts dark shadows. The effect can be softened with a diffuser, or 'bouncing' the light off a wall or ceiling.

Nearly all flash heads have a diffuser attachment to soften the light, and a tilt-swivel head for bouncing light off walls and ceilings is very common: bounce your flash off a coloured ceiling, however, and you may get a colour cast on the film. The lighting effects given by different techniques is shown below. Guns may also include a zoom head, adjustable according to the focal length of lens in use.

Direct

Diffused

Bounced

Dedicated flashguns such as the Canon 300TL computer flash (right) are designed to match one specific camera, in this case the Canon T90. They automatically set the ISO film speed, shutter sync speed and the exposure, and a flash-ready light comes on when gun has re-cycled. With **automatic guns** you set the film speed and aperture, as on the Metz 45CT (far right) according to flash/subject distance. The Canon gun, among other refinements, will give exactly the right amount of flash needed to fill-in existing light. The **portrait** (below) was taken in existing light, the one on the right with the 300TL gun set to the flash fill-in mode.

Problems with flash usually occur when the gun is close to the lens and you shoot directly at the subject. Watch for reflections and flare from shiny surfaces (below), and cast shadows. The group (below, right) all have 'red-eye' because flash was level with subjects' eyes and reflected off the retinas. Also, overall lighting is uneven—flash cannot selectively light subjects at different distances.

5

▷ THEMES AND ◁
VARIATIONS
PORTRAITS

The relationship between the photographer and sitter, and the success of the portrait, depends on the self-confidence of the photographer—his or her ability to take charge and create an informal atmosphere. This depends, in turn, on the photographer having some preconceived idea of the end result. In short—it helps to know what you want. I try and do some preliminary reconnaissance, planning the session in advance, visiting the location if possible, with some idea of the pose. The sitter's character may suggest this. People in the public eye, for example, who are used to being photographed, often have a 'ready-made' image that they consciously project and, being used to the camera lens, are tolerably relaxed. Some sitters, like **actor Don Warrington**, left, are 'naturals' and respond easily to direction. I had seen him in these clothes some weeks beforehand and so had an idea of how the picture might turn out. The balance of broad, simple shapes and the relaxed pose contrast with the yellow shirt, which really sings out—I made the shot by daylight on Fuji film, which has a bias to yellow, and a 70mm lens. Exposure was fairly long, about ⅛–½th second.

PORTRAITS

All but the most camera-shy people, those, that is, who are not entirely relaxed but want to make a favourable impression, trust the photographer to achieve this. There may be some stiffness of pose, and an unrelaxed mood that is the photographer's job to alleviate. Some professional photographers— like dentists—use music to establish a harmonious atmosphere. Others resort to what Snowdon described as a 'nerve-racking stream of small talk', which does little to put the sitter at ease. Perhaps the best approach is to discuss the shot and explain what you are aiming for, and so make them feel involved and cooperative. Obviously, time is a great asset— portrait sessions **always** take longer than you anticipate, but time may not be on your side, particularly where you are shooting at the sitter's convenience.

Advertising executive, John Salmon (above), photographed during a very rushed portrait session in the boardroom. I wanted him to look as if he were about to sell me something. In the picture of **painter Peter Blake** (right), flash has created a blue cast from the coloured walls. Blake chose the position (because he likes the view) and I shot the picture with diffused, frontal on-camera flash on Ektachrome 100. Both shots taken with a Canon T90 and 300TL computer flash.

PORTRAITS

Powerful, undiffused flash can produce a high-key shot of great impact, but it is generally better to soften flash with a diffuser. Hard shadows are not flattering, especially in photographs of women, and I tend to use daylight whenever possible. Daylight has a wonderful, soft quality, and varies according to the time of day (see also pp. 126–7), the time of year and the hemisphere. The cold but gentle northern light lends its own atmosphere to the portrait on the following page, 102/103, while the portrait opposite was made in Portugal in a room with shutters, to control the strong sunlight outside. The differences are equally apparent in both sitters' skin tones, although this can be adjusted to a certain extent with filters. I used an 81A 'warm-up' filter for the picture below, shot in London which, on Fuji film, gives a slight glow to the skin. Hands are invariably an asset in portraiture, supportive elements that can make their own mute comment about a sitter's personality, or lend an air of repose. The hands (and paws) below work well together, assisted by a linking element—in this case the black sweaters that make a simple shape, and the ginger kitten—a bonus. The girls, **Milly and Tabby Gentleman**, were taken on a Pentax with a 50mm lens, at about 1/30th second at f/5.6. In the portrait opposite, there was sufficient illumination for a hand-held shot on Ektachrome HS (ISO 160), and an exposure of around 1/60th second at f/5.6 or even f/8, judging by the depth of field.

PORTRAITS

Pianist Jeremy Menuhin, photographed by light from a window, reflected by a white-painted door to the sitter's right. Space was limited, and to include the angular shapes of the piano I had to use a 28mm wide-angle lens. The film was Ektachrome 100 and the exposure—with the camera on a tripod—about ⅛th second at f/5.6.

PORTRAITS

Putting your subjects in the right position and the right frame of mind is half the battle. Don't ask them to 'ignore the camera'—nobody can do that—better, in fact, to make them aware and involved with the operation. In the picture below, I was working with a camera crew in the Lake District. The low-lying autumn sun produced dramatic lighting effects, needing a careful balance of exposure between highlight and shadow. I took several readings with a hand-held meter for this portrait of **cameraman Chris Bradley**, settling on $\frac{1}{500}$th second at f/3.5 on Ektachrome 100, with a Pentax and 50mm lens. The 'mug shot' of **journalist and author Chris Matthew** (and on p. 93) was made in his home, following his remark, "I prefer the sort of portrait where part of the face is obscured." I used Ektachrome 100 film, a Canon T90 at $\frac{1}{60}$th second at f/3.5. The double portrait against the light, of **writers Len Deighton and Eric Ambler** (seated) was made in the Carlton Tower Hotel, London. Both men are also experienced photographers. Ambler looked up and said drily, "Ah, contre-jour . . ." Additional light was bounced off a curtain. Exposure was about $\frac{1}{20}$th second at f/8 (for the sitters' faces) on Fujichrome 100 and a Canon T90.

GLAMOUR

Here is one of the more enjoyable yet challenging subjects in photography. Beauty photography is a regular category in photographic journals in general, and the glossy fashion magazines in particular, which advertise, among other things, products of the cosmetic and fashion industries, and supports many fashion photographers. It is a subject that has created a specialist approach and technique.

Yet, as with other categories of photography, the subject is all. A beautiful woman, skilfully made up, is about eighty per cent of the success of the picture—the rest is lighting, atmosphere and the rapport generated between photographer and model.

This is more important than it might at first appear. A relaxed atmosphere is the first requirement, and an attitude on the part of the photographer that inspires confidence and reflects admiration. This is vital if your model is inexperienced, and it helps if you take her into your confidence and explain the effects you are trying to achieve.

All the women photographed here and on the following pages are non-professionals, but they share to varying degrees beauty, poise, style, freshness and—a necessary but often overlooked element— humour.

Backlighting and subtle use of reflectors give a soft and delicate quality to glamour shots, especially if the source is daylight. Lace curtains (right) have diffused the light. Reflection comes from adjacent walls and bed coverings. Exposure was 1/60th second at f/5.6 on an Olympus OM2 using Ektachrome 100 film.

Sunlight through a window controlled with blinds, highlights the hair and creates a glowing, translucent effect. The light was also reflected off a white wall close to the girl's face. For shots like these, take careful readings from the face and let the highlights burn out. Exposure was 1/60th second at f/2.8 on a Nikon F-301 camera and Ektachrome 100 film.

GLAMOUR

In the section on portraits I made out a case for pre-planning and having some idea of the end result. Try basing your first beauty shots on pictures you have admired, or thought might be within your capabilities as a photographer.

Keep it simple. Use daylight, or any of the flash techniques previously described in studio lighting—perhaps a frontally-placed brolly and flash head. Daylight can be softer and more flattering, and you could use a 90mm portrait lens, helped by an 81A filter to warm the skin tones, or a soft-focus filter to diffuse features slightly.

Always emphasise where you can the characteristics special to each woman—her hair, perhaps, poise, profile, figure and dress sense. If your pictures compliment the sitter, they will also compliment your skill as a photographer.

Miss Tulipland, 1986, photographed in the Springfield Gardens, Spalding in Lincolnshire. There were one or two problems, here. The subject needed backlighting to make a contrast of highlight and shadow on the ruffles of her dress, and this meant the use of reflectors in preference to fill-in flash. Slight underexposure gave stronger colour to the tulips in the background. Sunlight was fleeting, and had to be grabbed when it appeared. There was a cold, spring wind, and Miss Tulipland had to maintain a cheerful expression while the reflectors

threatened to take off. Taken on a Nikon FA, 50mm lens, using Ektachrome 100 film. Exposure was 1/60th second at f/8.

Sense of fun combined with relaxed cooperation from beauty writer Leslie Kenton, photographed in the Mandarin Suite of the Swiss Cottage Holiday Inn, London. I wanted the comfortable nicely furnished setting offered by the hotel, to which Miss Kenton added her own mood of informality. Daylight was limited, in spite of a large window area, and I needed a fairly fast shutter to catch facial expressions and movement. I managed with 1/60th second at f/3.5. on a Canon T90, 35mm wide-angle lens and Ektachrome 100 film.

NUDES

As every photographer knows, nudes are difficult. They are difficult because you have to steer a course between art and eroticism. By art I mean a restrained approach in lighting technique, and by eroticism I refer to the added measure of sexual awareness that is inherent in all nude shots. Photographs of nudes appeal to men, and why not indeed? Although there are photographers who insist on the value of nude shots as assisting the study of shape and form. In other words, the life class.

Eroticism can be conveyed by the model's expression or by the use of clothing combined by light and shade. The more sexually explicit a pose becomes, the more it errs in the direction of pornography. Nude pictures are designed to stir the libido gently and to provoke admiration. The fact that many

A limited amount of light can make for a brooding atmosphere (below) which I created using daylight underexposed by at least two stops. The picture opposite was made by posing the model against a black cloth about 7m (23ft) from a large window, but in failing light. I used an 81C Cokin Filter smeared at the bottom with Vaseline, and shot the picture with a Nikon FA, 50mm lens, Ektachrome 400 film at about 1 second at f/8.

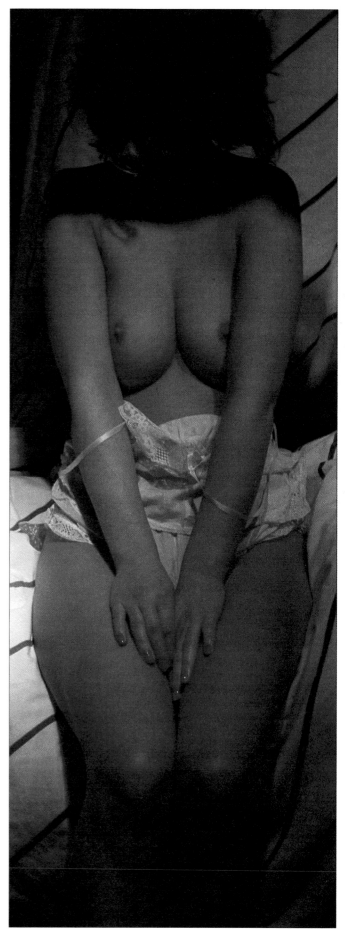

NUDES

photographers succeed in this is attested to by the pages torn out of photomagazines in public libraries: I hope that some of them are mine.

When lighting a nude, use a single light source and try to make the body blend in with the background as in the shot below. This helps to emphasise the form and adds to the mood of intimacy, and is the reason that group photo sessions with a nude model rarely produce good pictures. The girl on the right, relaxed on a bed, was photographed through a Venetian blind with the light from a single tungsten spot lamp, on Ektachrome tungsten film ISO 160. When you become more confident about photographing the nude body you can go for stronger lights, high-key effects and related backgrounds, especially in black and white with its wonderful tonal range.

Filters for nude shots can improve skin tones in black and white as well as in colour photography. Blue or green filters will darken skin with black and white, while red will lighten spots and blemishes. In colour, skin tones can be 'warmed up' with the 81 series. Soft focus filters come in various grades. You can also get a soft-focus effect by breathing on a skylight filter, or use the faintest smear of Vaseline.

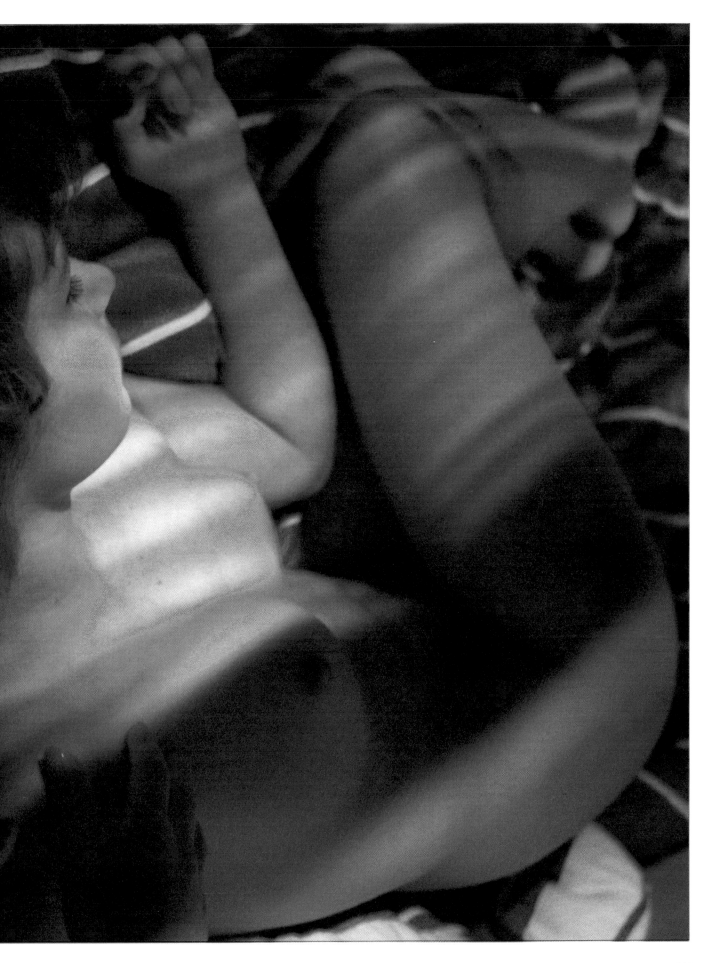

CROWDS AND GROUPS

CROWDS AND GROUPS

Colourful, expectant, curious, tense, watchful, joyful, angry; crowds are infinitely varied, and, as a source of pictures, what more could you want? You have to be some distance from a large crowd and slightly above it, to get a real impression of the excitement, anticipation and potential power that it evokes.

If you are part of a crowd, grab some candid shots—discreetly—when their attention is elsewhere, and you will be well rewarded with splendid examples of facial expressions and gestures, in particular at sports events. The ideal camera for this sort of photography is the rangefinder Leica or, better still, a compact, such as the tiny Minox 35ML.

The famous American photographer Weegee actually got every member of a huge crowd at Coney Island to look at his camera at the same moment. I cannot remember how he did it, fired a gun per-haps, but he took a memorable picture.

With groups this is easy, indeed essential if you are shooting a formal group where everyone should be clearly recognisable. The wedding shot below (part of the sequence on pp. 122–5) is a group that's nearly a crowd, but the picture is deliberately informal.

You may need a wide-angle lens, or the 28mm–35mm setting on a zoom, to include everyone in a widely spaced group where all participants have equal prominence. In the bottom picture, opposite, I was about 7m (23ft) from the group. Try to avoid having everyone facing bright sunlight, for they will be forced to squint. Better to use sidelight and expose to capture detail in the shadows. With smaller groups, you could use fill-in flash, a regular practice with professional photographers who leave nothing to chance.

Derby Day, Epsom 1986 (previous page), with a horse cantering towards the starting gate. Canon T70, with zoom lens on the 35mm setting and Ektachrome 100 film. It would have been better had I waited for the race, with all heads turned in one direction, but I wanted to get closer to shoot the action; it is the aim of all photographers to be in several places at the same time. The **informal wedding group**, (above), was made while the official photographer was setting up his camera (see also pp. 124–5) and the group (right) shot while anticipating a parade.

'EAP'—the Experimental Aircraft Program with pilot and film crew. The aircraft was due for take off, and I was given exactly two minutes to arrange the group. I shot from a low position to make a marginally more interesting composition. Nikon F-501 AF camera, 35mm lens, Ektachrome 100 film.

Wasdale Head, Cumbria. The pictures on this page were made for Kodak's 'Camera Angle' magazine. The climbing team and film crew, were shot from the top of a ladder, using an Olympus OM2, 35mm lens and Ektachrome 100 film. The figure fifth from the right, is Al Rouse, who died on K2 in 1986.

CHILDREN

The stages of growing up are many and transient. Children change and their clothes change, and later they begin to develop a self-consciousness that preludes maturity. Some children, though, will always be ready to pose, while others acquire a dislike of the camera and become restless and fidget and pull faces. Bribery usually works, and you in turn will have to work fast to get what you want. But children are generally wonderful subjects for the camera because of their natural charm and candour. The clichés about innocence and simplicity are accurate, though it can be difficult to steer a course between the innocent and the coyly sentimental. Very young children are really the subjects of 'candid' photography since you cannot expect them to hold a pose, and so you have to wait until the 'decisive moment'. It helps, though, to have a co-operative parent at hand (usually the mother of course) to induce the child to look in the right direction, and to strike up the interaction of liveliness that often produces splendid shots. The picture below of **mother and child** is a wonderful study, by John Salmon, of freshness and awareness, taken on an Olympus OM30, Kodak Tri-X film, at about 1/60th second, f/2.8. Daylight is the best source of lighting to enhance the softness of children's skin tones, used below and in the picture on the right. **Daisy Wallace, in a party dress**, was photographed by winter daylight through a window, and without a reflector, on Ilford FP3, with a Nikon F-501 AF camera. Compacts are excellent snapshot cameras but an SLR, especially an auto-focus SLR, will adjust to a child's rapid changes of position, and also keep a restless child intrigued (by the buzzing, clicking and bleeping) long enough to shoot off several frames before boredom sets in. Flash has this effect, too. It freezes action but the direct flash is too harsh for shots of children, and is better diffused or bounced off a white wall or ceiling. You can use flash for children's parties, but take into account the flash/subject distance and avoid the type of grouping where children in the foreground are overexposed while those in the background are dark (see p. 93).

CHILDREN

Anticipation is needed to catch expressions in children (above, right and below). A useful rule when photographing children is keep on the same level (opposite page) — physically and emotionally.

WEDDING DAY

For many, their wedding day is the most important day of their lives, and one that every guest is keen to record, judging by the number that bring cameras. If you want to make a picture essay you will have to get permission from the vicar or priest to take pictures inside the church. In most cases this is a simple formality and permission is usually granted, though flash is not acceptable. It is also an unattractive style of lighting for so romantic an occasion. Use flash only as a fill-in for shooting outside groups if the weather is dull or there's excessive contrast.

Assuming that you are not acting as the official wedding photographer, but are participating as a guest, your chance of a shot inside the church may be limited to the vestry, and when the bride and groom walk down the aisle at the end. Here, by pre-arrangement, the couple might stop and pose for a moment. The best you can hope for is ¹/₆₀th second at f/3.5 with a wide-angle 35mm lens and ISO 400 film. You need the wide-angle to include some of the church and congregation.

The most successful pictures are likely to be outside the church when, by tradition, bride and groom pose for the official photographer, with their immediate families, bridesmaids and so on. Don't get in the photographer's way; he will arrange the groups and you can ask if he—and they—mind you taking a few shots. A 35–70mm zoom will be useful here, to take in large groups and also some the church façade.

You will have plenty of opportunity at the reception to make your shots convey the pleasure and joy of the occasion. While the wedding photographer's shots will be formal, yours can be happily informal.

Signing the register in the vestry is a moment of relief and relaxation immediately following the marriage ceremony. If you are invited in with a camera, try for the romantic effects of daylight (far right) rather than flash (right). Light is usually through a small window, so you might get camera shake, as I did. Ask the couple to pose for **informal pictures** (opposite page) in addition to the more usual formal ones (below). Attractive backgrounds and surroundings will need to be included: try for a **group with the church**—I used a wide-angle lens—and unless you want to be part of the big **wedding group** get a panoramic shot of that, too.

WEDDING DAY

Ask the bride and groom if they will pose for the kind of picture on page 122—if you can get them away from the attentions of the guests; it's not easy! Be sure to snatch a picture of the cake-cutting ceremony, the toasts, the guests, perhaps a still-life of the gifts, a table of prepared food—anything that typifies or sums up the occasion.

Finally, the 'going-away' at the end. The shower of confetti, the furtive tear, the hugs and smiles, the ritual paraphernalia tied to the back of the car. You will need to take at least three cassettes of film to do justice to a major event that only the camera can successfully record.

Royal weddings are a quite different challenge, and a strategic camera position is essential if you are to get even one acceptable shot. The secret, I dis-covered, is to get there early—not hours early but three days early! I ignored this simple advice, with the result that heads got in the way (top right).

You absolutely have to be in the front of the crowd, with a long-focus lens on a monopod, and fast film. You have to place your camera in a posi-tion to ensure acceptable close-up shots of the procession. For security reasons you probably won't be allowed to use a collapsible step-ladder, so leave it at home. A favourite technique in shooting from crowds is to hold your camera above your head pointing at the main area of interest. It's hit-or-miss but, as added insurance, you could fit a wide-angle lens to your SLR—at least you'll get **something**.

Wedding receptions depend on seasons and therefore the weather, and if you attend an outdoor reception the conditions are ideal for photography. Don't miss the traditional shots, such as **Cutting the Cake** and the **Going Away**, the speeches and the toasts. For **Royal Weddings**, you need a lot of stamina and luck. Many of the on-lookers lined the route well in advance to obtain an uninterrupted view.

TIME OF DAY

Light that rakes a surface at an oblique angle reveals textural qualities previously dormant, creating irregular patterns of shadow and light where the surface is itself irregular. Early morning sunlight has this effect on cityscapes and landscapes and, as the sun climbs higher, the shadows shorten and the texture disappears. Towards the end of day, as the light fades, shadows blend together and the landscape softens.

Atmospheric effects help towards this diffusion of light due to moisture in the air, noticeable in the evening and early morning when ground mists lie low. Higher, in the mountain ranges, the air is crisp and clear but ultraviolet light may be a problem.

Some wonderful effects are created by the rising or setting sun. You may have to wait for hours, even days, for the ideal combination of light and atmosphere. Bear in mind, though, that such effects are transient and can disappear while you are fumbling with your tripod or loading film. I missed the most awe-inspiring sunset I have ever seen, or am likely to see, while driving across Cumbria, because I couldn't set my camera up in time before the sun slipped away. Anyway, it was a lesson well learned. Anticipate, keep calm, and try to be a step or two ahead of nature.

Corfe Castle, Dorset, at sunset. The solemn stillness is emphasised by soft light, haze and smoke from fires. Taken on a Nikon FA camera and 135mm lens with Ektachrome 100 film.
New England morning in the fall (below) in the clear air of hilly country. Shot with a Pentax Spotmatic and 50mm lens on Ektachrome 100 film.

TIME OF DAY

Market Square, Petersfield, Hampshire, dawn until dusk. Stallholders arrive first, the vicar (on his bicycle) at 8 a.m. At 11.00 a Punch and Judy show performed for the children. It was a Saturday in June, so there was a wedding—and contrasty lighting. The market had cleared by 6 p.m. Lights come on in the square by 9.00. Shot on a Canon T90, mostly at 28–35mm. Fujichrome 100 film.

TIME OF DAY

Any time of the day is suitable for photography, and practically all weather conditions will give you plenty of scope for good pictures. Take a broad view and think in terms of black and white as well as colour. I know that landscapes of delicate hues and faded colours beg the interpretation of colour film and perhaps sympathetic filtering, but look for contrast, shape and detail, and think also in black and white.

Some photographers hold with the view that the best time of day is early morning and towards sunset, and are fairly definite in their condemnation of noon as a bad time for picture taking. I disagree. High noon during the summer season in many parts of the world promises shots of vivid brilliance of colour and sharp detail. Look at the clarity of the three top pictures on the opposite page, all shot at midday or slightly later, compared with the softer and more diffused remaining shots on this spread, taken in early morning or late evening. In the noonday sun, haze is minimal, colour richer and detail finely etched.

Northumberland, early morning and late evening (top, left and right) in midsummer. The sun's position dramatically alters the landscape, and the colour, and eliminates the horizon in the second picture. **Morning mist in Dorset** creates ghostly beams of light, while the same morning mist in **northern Spain** lies low in the valleys beneath an overcast sky. Canon T70, Nikon FA, Pentax ME. All on Ektachrome 100 film.

Noonday sun at
Brighton
(far left),
**Fathepur Sikri,
India** (above) and
Paphos, Cyprus
(left). Below,
Wild Wales in
February, 4 p.m.

LANDSCAPES

High winds and spring sunshine, Kenwood, Hampstead. To capture the blurred foliage I used a tripod, a Pentax camera and two filters—a polarising and a X2 neutral density filter. The film was Fujichrome 50, and I bracketed exposures around 2–3 seconds at f/16.

LANDSCAPES

When the English painter Turner saw a storm gathering over the Yorkshire moors, he rushed out with his easel to celebrate the event on canvas. He sought atmosphere, drama and movement in landscape, and above all the effects of light. These are the qualities valued by the photographer, too, for landscape pictures—whether they are paintings or photographs—benefit from that extra element that gives them substance and interest.

Yet one may sit for hours in a landscape without the reward of a single grain of inspiration. Landscape photography is rather like angling. Quiet, introspective, dedicated, patient, yet demanding quick responses when the need arises.

To give yourself as much scope as possible means covering a lot of ground, preferably walking or cycling. Put the time of day on your side—taking advantage of the wonderful atmospheric effects of early morning or around sunset. Take advantage of stormy weather, especially sunshine and showers—a single shaft of sunlight in an otherwise stormy scene creates a magical touch.

Landscapes are more influenced by the quality of light than any other factor, apart from camera position, so find the most striking viewpoint and one that unites all the features into a coherent whole.

Passing summer storms and diffused light produce landscapes of delicate pastel shades and a range of hues at the blue end of the spectrum. This thatched cottage, in Norfolk, is plumb in the middle of a sea of golden barley. I could have dropped the cottage to the bottom of the picture and included a lot of sky, or taken the horizon to the top and had the cottage compete with the field. The compromise, above, offered a suitable balance, but the best solution was to change the camera position, zoom in, and frame the cottage through the trees (right).

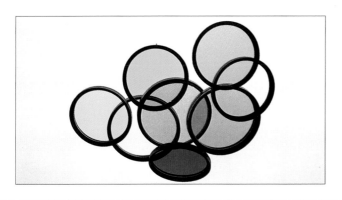

Filters for landscape. With black and white film, orange and yellow filters will darken blue skies and water. A yellow filter will give a more natural effect to a pale sky, and the more you move towards red, the darker the sky will become. A No. 25 red, or a deep red, will give you white clouds and black skies. Green filters lighten foliage and give a more contrasting dispersion of tones. With colour film, a polariser will darken a blue sky and enrich colours and a UV will marginally reduce haze. Graduated filters will colour select areas of a picture, while a neutral density will increase exposure times without affecting colour.

LANDSCAPES

Dealing with space and a panoramic view such as the one below, is a challenge easily ignored. After all, where is the point of interest, the dominant feature that conveniently leads the eye into and around the picture? Colour might help, but this picture was shot in black and white. What, then, has the subject to commend it to the camera?

Space, for one thing. Depth for another. These have endowed the scene with a quietness and serenity, helped by perspective and depth of field from a medium wide-angle lens, and the finely-rendered detail that leads the eye to the distant hills. It has a splendid 'get-away-from-it-all' quality that inspires the best travel posters. Because it was shot in black and white, the picture emphasises tonal values and fine detail less pronounced in colour.

Whether you shoot in black and white or in colour, look for unifying elements—light, space, detail, cloud effects or anything unusual in texture and shape. Work with the light—and against it. Take shots daringly underexposed (with slide film); use reflections in pools and lakes. Use a polarising filter to enrich colour. A well attested technique is to apply the rule of thirds. Select your point of interest, and compose your picture so that this point lies one-third in from either edge of the frame.

Wide open spaces invariably offer something of pictorial interest. John Freeman's landscape (opposite page), shot in Scotland, may have seemed fairly empty at first glance, but with black and white fine-grain film the detail and range of delicate tones in the foreground leads the eye into the picture. A wide-angle lens has given perspective to the clouds and a polarising filter has darkened the sky. Look for opportunities to **manage space** (above and left) by dividing it symmetrically or zooming in on sections, and noticing how light can **break up areas** (left) into patches of light and shade. Do not overlook seemingly bleak industrial areas—the pollution behind this French town has given a delicate orange cast to the scene and there is plenty of detail within the picture. Pictures above and left, Nikon FA and F-501 AF; below, Pentax Spotmatic. All on Ektachrome 100 film.

NIGHT LIGHTS

After dark may seem a less-than-encouraging time to shoot pictures, since the medium of photography is light, but with fast films and wide apertures, there is often enough light in cities to get pictures without having to use a tripod—both shots on this page were made with hand-held cameras.

With a tripod you can make exposures long enough to turn night into day, but the purpose of shooting at night is to capture the effects of artificial lighting, of reflections on rain-wet streets and the often spectacular streaks of light caused by passing traffic.

Fireworks are always a rewarding subject. You will certainly need a sturdy tripod, for exposures may be as long as 4 minutes or more, but you won't need fast film—in fact, the slower the better. Stop down to f/11 and follow the technique described in the caption below for the kind of results overleaf.

For a large display, wait until you can judge through your lens the 'ceiling', or height limit, reached by the bursts. It will be too late to move your position, so cover yourself by taking a wide-angle lens, or a zoom with a choice of wide angles of view.

For floodlit buildings and similar objects, you may need the sensitivity of a hand-held meter. If you get a TTL reading (probably around ¼–½ second at f/11) bracket over a two-stop range either side of the metered reading.

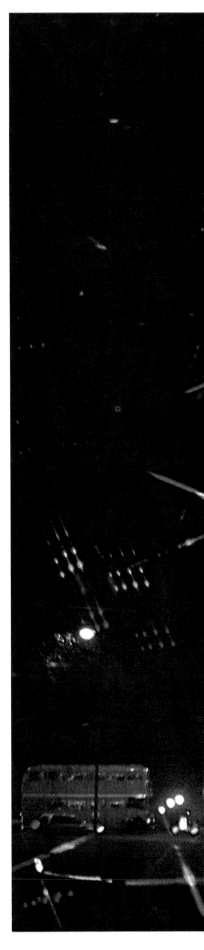

In Reno, Nevada, the sidewalk is actually carpeted in places. This was shot with a Praktica, hand-held, on Ektachrome HS (ISO 160) and a 35mm lens. Probably ⅟₆₀th second at f/2.8. **Hyde Park Corner, London,** (right). Special effects filters are more of a novelty than anything else, and they should be used with restraint. The diffraction, or starburst, filter here has given a slight touch of fantasy to an otherwise prosaic subject. The film is Fuji RSPII, 1600 reversal and the filter a Cokin Chromo-filter.

Firework display, London (following page). The picture was shot from Waterloo Bridge, which was lined with spectators—mostly photographers—and I used a Nikon FA with a Tamron 35–210mm lens mounted on a tripod. The film was Fuji 50 reversal, and the exposure about 4 minutes at f/11. During the exposure I 'dodged' out St. Pauls with my hand to prevent overexposure and also covered the lens with my hand between bursts. Keen observers will notice slight camera shake due, perhaps, to the heavy traffic crossing the bridge.

BUILDINGS

Is it asking a lot of a camera to capture the vertical sweep of the Eiffel Tower at a glance, to sum up in essence the monumental solidity of Egypt's pyramids, the soaring heights of New York's skyline, the glory that is Rome? Can an SLR, not to mention a compact, cope with the Colosseum or squeeze into the 35mm format the dignity of St. Peter's?

Reduced to two dimensions and the confines of an enprint, architectural shots may fail to measure up to their potential and promise. For the majority of us, famous and classic buildings represent the character and spirit of a place—as the Kremlin does for Russia, and the Taj Mahal for India—and we can consider ourselves fortunate if, while we were there, the light at the time of day was particularly favourable and illuminated the building with dramatic effect, or atmospheric conditions contributed to mood and moment.

Freedom of movement is the greatest advantage, giving you opportunity to change focal lengths and, therefore, angles of view. Easy with the little church, below, but a problem in confined city streets, right.

Mountain chapel at Brand, Austria, and by way of contrast the **Lloyd's building** in the City of London. Lloyd's 'futuristic' design is not easy to photograph because it is narrowly confined, I walked around it and finally settled for this reflection in a window. Canon T90, 28mm lens, Ektachrome 100 film.

BUILDINGS

When we look upwards at a tall building, the vertical lines appear to converge and taper, due to laws of perspective, laws not especially favourable to photography: with certain lenses, notably the wide-angle family, and from low viewpoints, the perspective is exaggerated. By tilting the camera backwards to include more of a building, the film plane is no longer parallel to the subject, and the effect is to make the building appear to fall over.

Professional photographers use a shift lens (below) to correct perspective. These are adjustable, 'shifting' the lens off its axis and, in so doing, correcting perspective distortion. Shift lenses are expensive, but they can be hired. If you process your own prints, a degree of correction can be carried out in the darkroom by tilting the enlarger head or printing frame until vertical lines are parallel. Correction, however, can only be minimal since the image tends to stretch (see comparative pictures below). You may have to make some adjustments to the exposure of parts of the print.

In some cases, distortion doesn't matter, and may be acceptable in shots of modest buildings, as the garage below illustrates. Alternatively, you can accentuate distortion by moving in close and exploiting the dynamic—and controversial—lines of modern structures, as I attempted to do with the Lloyd's building (previous page).

If you have time—photography's most vital commodity next to light—explore your subject from different camera positions and with a variety of focal lengths. Converging verticals are less acute as you move back from a building, and from a distance you can use a long focus lens.

Country garage in red, white and blue, shot with a 28mm wide-angle lens. Vertical distortion is inevitable in buildings shot from low levels, unless you use a shift lens (below). If you want to photograph buildings without traffic or pedestrians obscuring the detail, try a long exposure: **Southgate tube station** (opposite page), a gem of 1930s London Transport architecture, was photographed during a busy weekday at midday. By combining ×2 and ×4 neutral density filters (which absorb light), I was able to give an exposure of several seconds. The effect has been to wipe out all but two figures, and most of the passing traffic.

Canon tilt and shift lens In addition to correcting perspective, the lens has also shifted my reflection from the door of the gallery (opposite page) and out of the picture. The lens will also tilt to maximise depth of field.

BIRD WATCHING

Patience and the time to sit behind your camera for hours, are the first two requirements of wildlife photography. Birds are easily the most familiar and accessible form of wildlife, depending on location and season, of course. Photographers with a garden can attract a variety of birds by siting a feeding table near the house, and near to a convenient window so that you can shoot from within.

To get an image of reasonable size on your film you will need a lens of at least 200mm at about 5m (16ft) from the table. Using, say, Kodachrome 200 film (a compromise of grain and speed) you will get $^1/_{125}$th second at between f/5.6 and f/8 (for depth of field). At this speed you will also need a tripod and cable release—or a remote control firing system—and preferably a camera that has automatic film advance and aperture-priority automatic exposure.

You will not need a fast shutter, catching birds in flight is a specialist technique, but aperture priority is useful in case there's a change in the light. The electronic noises-off performance of an autofocus, auto-wind camera may scare away shy birds, but you could try muffling your camera with a padded cover.

Photographers working in the field will need a 'hide'. You can buy portable ones, but all you really need is a simple frame covered by lightweight waterproof fabric, suitably camouflaged. A slit in the fabric is sufficient to poke your lens through and obtain a view of the subject and approach path. Garden birds can be enticed with food. Others have regular habits and perches and may sit still just long enough for you to grab a shot—if you have patience.

Bird pictures fall into two categories: shots in flight (opposite) and shots of stationary birds. To freeze a flying bird you need electronic flash. To photograph perched birds, a long lens and a hide are essential. I spent hours in a Dorset garden crouched behind a 500mm lens to shoot the birds on this page. The **robin** was attracted to cereal sprinkled on the statue's head.
Flycatchers (left) habitually used the same branch so I could prefocus on one spot, others were caught before seeing the camera, a Nikon FA. Film was Agfachrome 100.

Specialist photographers who capture flying birds on film set themselves stern conditions of image quality. The camera must freeze the action completely, although a slight blurring of the wing tips, to suggest speed, is acceptable. There must be a reasonable depth of field and a close-up image—the kingfisher (below) fulfils these requirements and is a good example of the results of in-flight photography, made by Hugh Clarke.

How do you arrest the movement of a kingfisher, whose wings probably exceed 30 beats a second and in that time will cover a distance of 13m (42ft), and what kind of camera and film do you use? Bird photographers favour the 35mm format, partly because of the detail and permanence of Kodachrome films and the suitability of the focal plane shutter on the SLR camera, plus the choice of viewing screens, motor drives and, on some models, electronic remote control.

The main consideration, though, is electronic flash. As Clarke explains, a flash speed of between $\frac{1}{17,000}$th and $\frac{1}{20,000}$th second is needed to freeze the wings of a small bird in flight, using an aperture of f/8 to f/16 on a 135mm lens. A longer focal length is unnecessary because the camera is sited in a hide about 3m (10ft) from the bird's flight path, and three flash heads about 1m (3ft) from the path.

Clarke's flash is powered by a capacitor with a quite lethal output of 375 joules, and the heads are sited one either side of the camera and one above and slightly to one side of the subject, all well protected against damp and rain. The flash is triggered by a light beam aimed at a photoelectric cell. The bird breaks the beam across its path and the light pulse is converted to an electrical pulse that fires the shutter via a solenoid.

A lot of methodical preparation is needed, including aligning the light beam, checking connections, and deciding exactly where to focus. This depends on the 'aim-off' factor, which must take into account the distance the bird has travelled after breaking the beam and before the shutter fires: the camera has to be focused at a point about 15cm (6in) beyond the beam. Correct focus and aim-off are arrived at by running a test film.

CAR AND DRIVER

Such is our preoccupation with cars that they seem to be a natural subject for photography, along with snapshots of family and friends, and records of holidays and celebrations. I have photographed all the cars I have ever owned and, at *concours d'elegance* shows and race tracks, cars I would like to own.

At race tracks, the panning technique will give your car shots an impression of speed, slightly blurring car and background. An ideal camera for this type of picture is an autofocus with continuous servo. Set your shutter for ¹⁄₂₅₀th second and pan smoothly with your camera, hand-held, flowing through the movement as the car passes, or bracket shutter speeds from ¹⁄₁₂₅th to ¹⁄₅₀₀th second to give yourself a choice of effects.

A good vantage point is often on a bend, where you can get head-on shots of cars as they come straight towards you, dramatically filling the viewfinder. For this you will need a long focus lens of more than 200mm (or 200mm plus a converter) and a tripod to prevent camera shake.

Practice day, when many race tracks are clear of crowds, offers excellent vantage points for panning shots and close ups. You will need at least a 200mm lens to make it worthwhile, and fast film. This picture, of John Charles driving a 1956 'C' type Connaught at Silverstone was shot with a Nikon F-501 AF on a 70–210mm zoom, using Ektachrome 400 film. The shutter speed was ¹⁄₂₅₀th second.

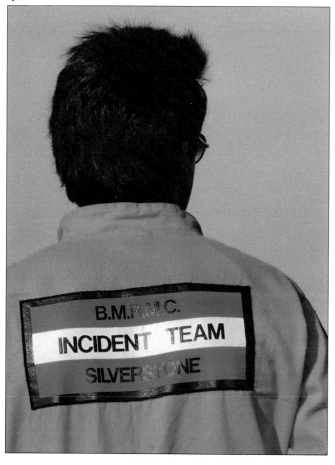

CAR AND DRIVER

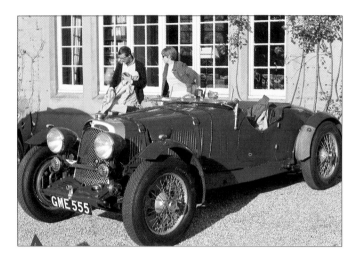

Classic cars are subjects of serious study and investment — they also produce rewarding photographs and almost abstract studies of light and shadow (above and right). Adding a driver brings an otherwise static subject to life, especially if the driver is **Stirling Moss**, here photographed with the marque with which he is mostly associated — Mercedes Benz, the 300SL Gullwing. I used a Canon loaded with Ektachrome 100. Although it was rather dark I chose to avoid flash and got about ¼5th second at f/3.5, while leaning out of a window. **Le Mans** provided a study of French police and a Porsche before the start of the race. I shot this on a long lens from the press box. It is almost impossible for members of the public to get a pass for the track or pits, but you can get to good shooting positions if you pay and/or get there early.

SPORTING LIFE

At any sporting event worthy of news coverage you'll see the press photographers who are allowed to shoot more or less anything they want, provided that they don't get in the way of the action. This is often fast paced, sometimes punctuated by spectacular incidents, which the really tuned-in photographer anticipates and grabs when the chance comes along.

Fast film, a 200mm lens on your SLR camera, and perhaps a monopod will set you up as a sports photographer. Not of professional status perhaps, but if you have a sharp eye, fairly fast reflexes and a knowledge of sporting events, you have as good a chance as the professional of catching some exciting moments.

At crowded events you will have to get there early to obtain a strategic field of view; even portraits and candid shots of sportsmen and women are quite feasible if you can get near enough.

Test cricket at Lords (above) and racing **yachtsman Chay Blyth** in Plymouth Sound (right). Sports photography doesn't have to be all action, although I was in an ace of being seasick before I took the shot of Blyth, with a Pentax, a 35mm lens and Ektachrome 100 film.

SPORTING LIFE

A day at the races can satisfy the needs of the most exacting enthusiast. Follow the jockeys to the starting gate for the tense moments before they're off (below). Follow the 'get there early' rule, if you can, and explore the track for strategic camera positions. A good place is against the rail and on a bend. There, you can catch a shot of the horses as they come straight towards you, dramatically filling your long lens. It may help to prefocus on a spot if your camera is not of the AF type, and trip the shutter the instant they come into your focused zone.

Try low angle shots. Take a pair of lightweight steps and try high angle shots above the heads of the crowd. Shoot the crowd, too: the bookmakers, the punters, the trainers and jockeys. Some race courses allow the public freedom to move around, others are stricter and more enclosed. At the Epsom Derby, for example, you can get excellent views almost around the entire course—I was once able to photograph the Royal Family, all standing in a line,

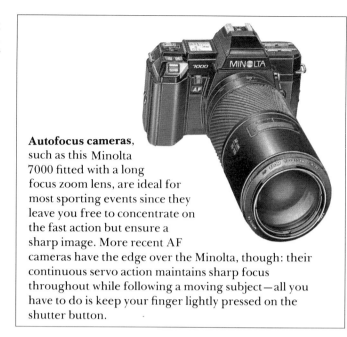

Autofocus cameras, such as this Minolta 7000 fitted with a long focus zoom lens, are ideal for most sporting events since they leave you free to concentrate on the fast action but ensure a sharp image. More recent AF cameras have the edge over the Minolta, though: their continuous servo action maintains sharp focus throughout while following a moving subject—all you have to do is keep your finger lightly pressed on the shutter button.

from a position close by the press stand, using a 200mm lens. You'll need at least 200mm and ⅟₅₀₀th second to catch horses and riders, so take fast film, ISO 400, and a monopod for extra support.

Climber Dave Armstrong pioneering a hard route up Great Gable on Scafell, Cumbria. Olympus OM2 with 200mm lens, Ektachrome 100.

The highest point on earth. This is the kind of shot you absolutely have to get right—there's unlikely to be a second chance. Norwegian Everest team on the summit, 1986, photographed by Chris Bonington, Olympus OM1 24mm lens on Kodachrome 25. The OM1 is the only camera not to seize up in sub-zero temperatures, and Bonington usually takes 2 OM1 bodies to high altitudes. In snow scenes, camera meters are inclined to underexpose to compensate for brightness. TTL meters are calibrated to respond to the medium tones (18–20 percent grey) in average subjects. "I tend to ignore the meter at altitude with a lot of snow around," writes Bonington, "and bracket close ups of figures with the sun on them at around ⅟₂₅₀th second at f/5.6 and slightly more distant group shots like this one at around ⅟₂₅₀th at f/8, then one on either side."

SPORTING LIFE

When covering events, it helps to have some knowledge of the sport, or at least an idea where the action is likely to take place. So, position, anticipation and a certain amount of luck are all needed.

While you may not have the freedom of the press in the stadium and race track, there's still plenty of scope for getting good shots from the public areas. Give yourself a chance to get as near to the action as possible—or the impression of being there by using a long focus lens so that you can fill the frame of your picture. Some sports—horse racing for instance—can mean long periods of waiting interspersed with brief flurries of activity, so you've time to prepare, check the distance, the point of focus, the exposure and constantly check that the film is winding on. If you are using slide film, make regular exposure checks too, preferably with a hand-held meter. A long focus or zoom lens around 135mm and above will mean camera shake, unless you use fast shutter speeds or mount your camera on a support (see Exposure). To freeze the action, you'll need at least ½250th second and above, depending, of course, on the sport. Panning with the subject gives an impression of speed, or use slower shutter speeds: this means mounting your camera on a monopod or tripod. Watch the pros in action, most use rugged Nikons or Canons with motor drive attachments and weighty lenses supported on a monopod. They need a wide aperture of around f/2.8 on lenses with a focal length of 300mm and above, and such lenses cannot be hand-held. If your camera has an integral motor drive, or you fit a motor drive attachment, use it with caution or you'll soon run out of film. Motorised units are in two categories: the motor wind, which advances the film automatically, and is a built-in feature of several SLRs, and the motor drive, which is featured on Canon's T90 and Nikon's 301 and 501 and as an accessory for many other cameras. Motor drives advance the film rapidly—Canon's amazing F-1 will whip the film through at 14 frames per second, the T90 at 4.5 fps, while Nikon's 501 is paced at 2.5 fps. In fact, a motor wind at 2 to 3 fps is quite sufficient for all but the most dramatic incidents on the Grand Prix circuit: in most sporting events as I have said, the action is brief and peaks for only a few seconds. Firing at around 2 to 3 frames per second will give you at least a dozen shots that cover the action, and at least one of these should be acceptable. It may even be the sports picture of the year . . .

Four methods of dealing with a fast ball are—shoot it, hit it, catch it, or get out of the way. Nikon FA camera, 500mm Nikkor mirror lens, about ½500th second at f/8 on Ektachrome 400 film.

School sports are no different from any adult sporting occasion—all the drama, anguish, rivalry and audience reaction are there for the taking. Some events run concurrently with others so you'll need to know the programme in advance to plan your priorities. A long lens will enable you to get close-up shots of hurdlers as they leap towards you, of last-gasp runners breasting the tape, of high-jumpers arching over the bar, or of exhausted competitors prostrate on the turf. You will certainly be asked for pictures, so take your shots on fast print film such as ISO 400, and if you have the advantage of two cameras, use one for colour and the other for black and white. If one of your cameras is a compact, save it for non-action pictures, the prize-giving ceremony, for example, and candids of people.

Sports Day at Langley Grammar School, Buckinghamshire. There are more events than one photographer can adequately cope with, but don't overlook the referee, the school staff, the supporters and the prize-giving ceremony. The fast-paced action may use up a lot of film. All shots taken on a Minolta 7000, 70–200mm zoom and Ektachrome 100 film.

HADRIAN'S WALL

The ancient monument known as Hadrian's Wall stretches in broken patches from Newcastle-upon-Tyne over 70 miles to Carlisle, across undulating countryside of clear, panoramic vistas and wild beauty.

The area is much visited by tourists, populated by shaggy sheep and piping birds—and little else. In a sense it has always been a no-man's land—even as late as the 18th century a military road was built along its southern length, and much of the Wall's stone was used as hard core by army surveyors.

It would take four seasons to make a thorough picture essay of the Wall, but I was limited to only a week during summer. The Wall seemed an appro-priate and challenging subject for a picture essay since it passes through industrial areas, suburbs, a city centre, and then by-passes most towns and villages as it wanders across the hills and crags, by rivers and lakes, forest and woodland.

Explorers usually begin at Wallsend near New-castle and travel westwards. I didn't know this, and cycled eastwards from Carlisle, but it makes little difference from which end you start—a photo essay is a visual chronicle of landscape, people, natural history, and anything else that takes your fancy on the way, coming or going.

This is the sort of project available to every mobile photographer, depending of course on the suita-

Above Greenhead (previous page) the road swings towards the Roman fort at Carvoran where there is a Roman army museum, and also one of the best preserved stretches of the Wall. 35mm lens, polarising filter. **School outing** (above) by the River Eden at Warwick Bridge near Carlisle.

Irthing Bridge (left) near Brampton. To emphasise the already rich brown colour of the river I used a Cokin Gradual T1 filter over a 35mm lens. **Buttercups and daisies** (right), by Milecastle 48 at Gilsland. Milecastles are counted from Newcastle, and there were originally 80 along the Wall, one for each Roman mile. At Gilsland, as elsewhere, only the foundations remain.

HADRIAN'S WALL

bility and scope of your surroundings. When embarking on a picture essay, make your shots have continuity, yet be flexible in your approach—an essay should sum up the essence of time and place. Take a limited amount of equipment (but plenty of film), camera, wide-angle, standard and medium tele lenses, or zoom equivalents. Take a tripod, and a few filters. Top of the list is a polarising filter, one or two graduated filters of the Cokin type, and yellows and reds for black and white film. I shot the entire essay with a Canon T70 camera and Fuji-chrome 100 film.

Three men in a boat on Crag Lough. One of a series of bracketed shots, exposing for the highlights to create a silhouette and to capture detail on the surface of the water. Exposure, was probably about ¹/₁₀₀₀th second at f/16. **Curlew country** (left). Curlews are everywhere, their piping, warbling cry the only sound in an otherwise still landscape. Panned with a 200mm lens. **Flora and fauna** (right). Natural and agricultural details give a more intimate study of a subject, and balance the broader view. The Wall is a national monument, all but the eastern end goes through farmland, given to grazing for sheep, like this Scotch Blackface.

HADRIAN'S WALL

Vanishing points and dynamic linear perspective (opposite page, top left and right) give depth to pictures as the eye naturally follows the receding lines. The train to Newcastle passes the Milecastle at Gilsland, and at Winshields the Wall threads as a dry, grey ribbon over grassy crags. **White house** near Thirlwall Castle, caught by afternoon sun, makes a dominant feature in a gentle landscape of grazing meadows. 200mm zoom lens.

Tourists at Housesteads fort (top) and a view looking towards Housesteads from Cuddy's Crags. Stretches of the Wall are turf-covered and you can walk along the top. When the wall was built, between 78 and 84 AD, it was 6 meters (28ft) high, and measured 80 Roman miles (73 statute miles). In few places today is the Wall higher than 2 meters (6½ft) but it is, after all, nearly 2000 years old.

HADRIAN'S WALL

Wall walkers at Heddon on the Wall (top), doing the route from Newcastle westwards, the traditional way, although I did it eastwards from Carlisle. The landscape is very hilly, the inns and hotels few and far between. Would they be smiling, I wondered, by the time they reached Carlisle? The Wall at Heddon is one of the first (or last) substantial examples.

Power station on the Tyne (above) from near Heddon. The countryside gives way fairly abruptly to the urban spread of Newcastle, and the Wall gives way abruptly to modern brick, and the terrace houses of Dunton (right). It is an impressive juxtaposition of ancient and modern. The final stones of the Wall are in the Swan Hunter shipyard at Wallsend.

6

DEVELOPING
▷ AND PRINTING ◁

The picture that you visualised and then captured on film is only part of the photographic process. The rest is carried out in the darkroom or colour laboratory, and for the many photographers who do their own printing, this is the most rewarding—and magical—aspect of the entire procedure.

Most homes have somewhere that can be converted into a darkroom and made light-tight, but must have the facilities of running water and electricity.

You will need basic equipment. An enlarger, preferably one including a head for colour; developing trays and chemicals. Whether you work in black and white or produce your own colour prints and slides, you will find that with experience you gain greater control over the image, and eventually over the quality and impact of your pictures.

DEVELOPING AND PRINTING

Both black and white print films, and colour print films—as distinct from slide films—go through two identical stages. After you remove the film from the camera it must be developed, and this process give you the reversed-tone image, or negative. You use your negative to obtain a positive print on photographic paper. The two processes can be carried out at separate times.

Developing a film
A negative is produced by immersing the film in three separate chemical solutions, in sequence, and in a light-tight tank. The first is the developer which reveals the latent image, registered on the film at the moment of exposure in the camera. The development is then halted (it would otherwise continue naturally) by adding the second 'stop' solution, and finally the fixer solution which makes the image permanent.

To develop a film you will need: a timer; developing tank and spiral; thermometer; calibrated mixing jugs of adequate capacity; film clips, and the processing chemicals. Pre-

pare as much as you can in advance. If chemicals are re-usable, such as stop bath and fixer, keep them in stoppered plastic bottles ready for use. Developers are more sensitive and must be prepared at exactly the right temperature, and the film must be developed for exactly the right amount of time, according to maker's recommendations.

Some developers can be mixed with water and re-used several times. Others are of the 'one-shot' type, to be discarded after use. There are many available, some as solutions, some in powder form, designated for fast film, fine grain, high or low contrast. To start with, try one-shot solutions until you are familiar with the processing technique. Later on, try mixing up powdered developers, which are generally re-usable and economical.

Loading the film
Film has to be taken out of the cassette and loaded into the tank in total darkness. It is easier to feed the film into the spiral if you round off the leader with scissors. You will be

doing this in the dark, so make sure everything is within easy reach.

Having loaded the tank and secured the lid, you can now switch on the light and start by pouring in the developer. As a rough estimate, it takes no longer than 20 minutes to load, develop and fix a film. After the fix has been poured off, the film can be removed from the tank and thoroughly washed in running water, before drying.

Hang the drying film in a cool, dust-free place with a clip-weight at one end. When dry, cut the film into convenient lengths until needed for a contact print, and later enlargement of negatives.

Making a print
Photographic paper is coated with an emulsion similar to that of a film; it is light-sensitive and yields an image during development. Papers are available in grades, to be used according to the density of your negative. Start off with a multi-grade paper, a sort of all-purpose type, to make a contact print and enlargement, following the guide.

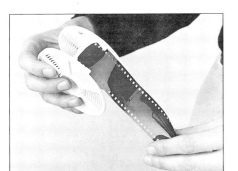

Remove the film from the cassette with a bottle-opener, or a special cassette opener—they are not expensive. With scissors, cut off the leader and trim the corners, this makes it easier to feed on to the spiral in the dark. It's a good idea to practise this a few times with an old length of waste film.

▼

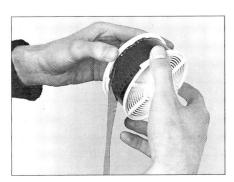

Wind the film on to the spiral, then cut off the spool.

▼

Put the loaded spiral into the film tank, secure the lid firmly in place. You can now take the tank into the light.

Prepare developer, stop bath and fixer as recommended by the makers.

Pour developer into the tank and activate the timer.

▽

Invert tank once, and tap it smartly to dislodge any air bubbles. Leave for about one minute. Then repeat the process of inverting and tapping. Repeat throughout the development time.

▽

Pour out developer 5 or 10 seconds before development time is due to end. Now pour in stop bath. Invert and agitate as before. Do the same with the fixer, leaving film in for the required time.

Pour out fixer. This ends the chemical processing. Your film should now be washed for about 15 minutes in running water, and ensure washing is even. A soapy solution and a squeegy will see that there are no smears or drying marks. Hang, with a film clip to weigh it down, in a dust-free area.

▽

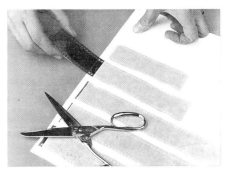

When your film is dry, cut it into even lengths and store in a negative sleeve.

▽

To make a contact print, prepare your processing solutions according to the maker's directions—the developer, stop bath and fixer should be at the correct dilution and temperature, and the trays conveniently placed.

Take a sheet of paper from the packet and lay it emulsion side up on the enlarger baseboard. Lay the strips of negatives down on the paper—emulsion to emulsion. Lay glass plate on negatives to keep them flat.

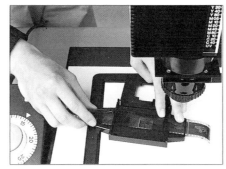

To enlarge one of your negatives, place the selected negative in the negative carrier, emulsion side down. Dust off negative and carrier with a blower brush. Place carrier in enlarger.

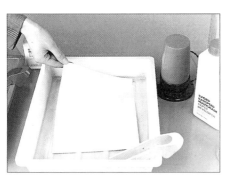

Expose to light from the enlarger, using a medium f stop of , say f/8.

Focus image on your enlarger at widest f stop, and at required size of enlargement. Turn off enlarger and load baseboard easel with paper, emulsion side up. Set a medium f stop of, say f/8.

You will need to experiment to find your overall best exposure, probably about 10 seconds. Remove paper, and slide it quickly into the developer tray. Agitate tray, rocking gently, and allowing the solution to wash over film for even development.

Assess contacts and choose negs for enlargement. If sheet is too dark, stop down the lens. If too light, open up the aperture.

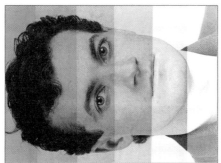

Make a test strip by covering about three-quarters of paper with card. Expose for 5 seconds. Slide card along to reveal next strip, and so on, until all paper has been exposed in timed strips, giving you a range of exposures from which to choose.

Remove from baseboard easel and develop, stop and fix as for contact sheet.

When enlarging, set the enlarger lens f stop so that an exposure time of between 10 and 20 seconds can be achieved. Too short a time can lead to problems in maintaining accuracy and does not allow for selective print control by 'burning' and 'dodging'. Too long a time can lead to risk of enlarger shake, and heat from the enlarger lamp may buckle or 'pop' the negative and throw it out of focus.

Burning and dodging are techniques where you use your hand to shield part of the print from light during exposure, holding back areas that are too dense and giving additional exposure to weak areas. By shaking your hand backwards and forwards you can feather the edge of the selected area. When contact printing and enlarging, make a test strip to save using a whole sheet of paper.

Learn to assess the density of negatives. A thin, underexposed negative, and a dense, overexposed negative will be harder to print than normally balanced ones. A thin negative may need a hard grade paper, a dense negative a soft paper. Negatives with good detail in the highlights (the dark areas of the negative) and detail in the shadows (light areas) will print well.

When image build-up is complete, remove print with tongs and slide it into the stop bath for about 30 seconds. Now slide print into the fixer. Leave for 2 or 3 minutes until fixed. Your print can now be viewed in normal light and is ready for washing.

The visible spectrum is made up of seven hues which combine to produce white light: when a narrow beam of daylight passes through a glass prism, it splits up into the spectrum. Using projector lamps and transmitting the beams through filters of the three primary colours—called the additive primaries—red, green and blue, we can produce white light by mixing them together. Project light through two filters only, and they will produce a third colour—the complementary. Red and green make yellow; red and blue make magenta; blue and green make cyan. Yellow, cyan and magenta are known as the subtractive primaries (shown on the right) because each colour transmits two others and **subtracts** a third. The 'tripack' layers of colour film are in effect filters of the subtractive primaries, as are the filters in a colour enlarger. Additive filters cannot be overlaid to produce colours, but subtractive filters can. Filters of partial density, used in pairs, will transmit all the colours to obtain a complete colour image in only one exposure.

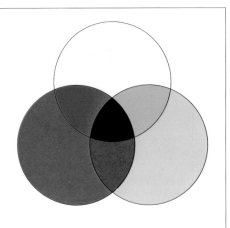

Colour prints from negatives and slides

Colour printing is as easy as printing in black and white, and you employ much the same technique, projecting your colour negative on to a sheet of colour print paper. Some experts advise having your film professionally processed to the negative stage, from where you take over to make your own prints.

With a good colour processing kit, you can do both developing and printing; I used the Paterson Colour Darkroom, principally aimed at beginners, and which includes all the equipment needed for developing your film to the negative stage, then making a print from the negative. I produced an acceptable print the first time I used it, without any previous experience of processing kits.

Durst, who make the famous range of enlargers, had a kit which included components from other manufacturers, components still separately available, but withdrew it when faced with price increases. This is the problem with all photographic equipment manufactured in Japan or Germany, and it hits hard at an already budget-conscious market.

Some photographic dealers have the facilities to give demonstrations of colour processing using a variety of makers' equipment. A popular up-market processor is the Jobo CPE2, an automatic machine with a rotary drum that maintains the correct temperature throughout the processing of films and prints. To this you would need to add an enlarger—it depends on whether you are starting from scratch, or wish to add colour processing equipment to the colour head you already possess.

So, using basic equipment, you can produce either colour prints from negatives, colour prints from slides, and you can develop your own slide film. The type of print depends on the paper and the process, also available in kit form. One of the finest is Agfacolor Process 70, giving rich blacks and clean whites and minimal filtration differences. The process is used with Agfacolor type 8 paper.

The main thing in colour printing is to maintain consistency, from exposure in the camera to the final print, especially in regard to enlarger filtration—maintaining consistency means that problems with colour casts are reduced to a minimum. Kodacolor films give consistent results on Ektacolor 78 paper, processed with the Ektaprint 2 kit.

In printing from slides, the chemistry is slightly different, and by far and away the best process is the up-to-date Cibachrome P30. The all in powder form chemicals are made into solutions by the user, producing vibrant, bold colours and an excellent range of tonal values. It has archival permanence, but is more expensive than competitors such as Kodak's Ektachrome R3 process with Ektachrome 22 paper.

Developing slide films

With a developing tank as part of your colour darkroom, you can process your own slide films. You will need a chemical kit for the E6 process, the same process that develops Ektachrome, Fujichrome and Agfachrome films. Kodachrome cannot be processed at home, because it employs a special chemistry where colour formers, or dyes, are added during development. Processing kits contain liquid concentrates to make up into three solutions—a black and white developer, a colour developer, and a bleach/fix. One of the most reliable kits is the Photocolor Chrome 6, or Paterson's 3E6; the Jobo automatic processor will also develop slide films with their own chemicals.

All you have to do is load the film into the tank as described on previous pages, or use the Jobo Daylight-Loading Tank, which enables you to feed the cassette into the tank without having to use the darkroom or a changing bag. Accurate temperature control is needed with E6 processing, but otherwise the business is quite straightforward and takes about 25 minutes to process a roll of film. The important thing in all colour processing is to follow the maker's instructions.

In colour printing, using the colour head of an enlarger, selective filtration will correct casts to give you a balanced print. Only two filters are needed, since three would filter out all the colours. By sliding a filter in the path of white light from the enlarger lamp—magenta, for example, you subtract blue and red, which reduces a green cast. Dial-in filters progressively increase or decrease the density of filtration, and the numbers on the filters correspond to this scale—10 cyan is a deeper colour than 5 cyan. Filters can be selectively added to achieve the same end result—instead of using magenta to subtract green, you can add yellow and cyan.

DEVELOPING AND PRINTING

Part of the equipment supplied in Paterson's Colour Darkroom kit. Chemicals are kept at the right temperature in a water bath. As in all film chemistry, where chemicals drop below the working temperature, you can correct development by increasing developing time. It is better, though, to try and maintain consistent temperatures and working methods.

The colour print processing sequence shown below and opposite is intended to give you an idea of the simple and straightforward methods of obtaining a picture from a colour negative. The Paterson kit is just one of several routes to a colour negative/positive print, or a print from a colour slide, but all processes are more or less the same.

You can build up your own colour darkroom, buying equipment from different makers—ask your photo dealer's advice, and look in the photo magazines, many of which regularly publish details of up-to-date equipment and techniques.

If you buy a colour processing kit, read the maker's instructions and follow them carefully—they have been thoroughly tested for (almost) foolproof results, and if you standardise your methods, your prints will be of consistently good quality.

 ▷   **IN NORMAL LIGHT**   ◁

Make up processing chemicals according to manufacturer's instructions, and keep them at the working temperature. Variations in the quality of results may be due to incorrect temperatures and inconsistent agitation.

▽

To make a colour print, load your negative in the negative carrier, and 'dial-in' the recommended filtration—for example, 45 yellow and 45 magenta.

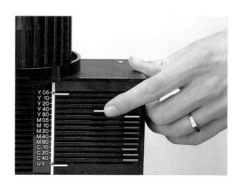

The process shown here used Kodacolor II negatives and Kodak Ektacolor 78 RC paper. Different negative films and colour papera will probably need different filtration in the enlarger.

▶   **IN TOTAL DARKNESS**   ◀

Load test strip printer with colour print paper. Turn on enlarger light and give progressive exposures—5, 10, 15 seconds, and so on.

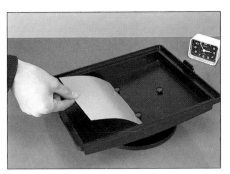

Slide paper into orbital processor and place lid firmly on until it clicks.

Agitate to ensure even development for recommended time—about 3 minutes.

You can now remove the lid from the processor and inspect the print.

▷ **IN NORMAL LIGHT** ◁

Pour warm water into orbital processor, leave 30 seconds, then pour away.

Pour in correct quantity of developer at recommended temperature.

Pour off developer, add water rinse. Pour away rinse, and add bleach/fix. Rotate processor for 2–3 minutes. Pour off bleach/fix.

Your test strip gives you a variety of exposures ranging from 5 to 25 seconds.

When the print is dry, select the best exposure time and make the final print according to the time and filtration of selected strip.

If the colour balance is poor, correct the filtration. A change of 05 will give you a slight colour shift, while a change of 40 gives a considerable shift.

FILTER CORRECTIONS PRINTING FROM NEGATIVES

Colour Cast	Subtract	Or add
blue	yellow	cyan + magenta
green	magenta	yellow + cyan
red	cyan	yellow + magenta
yellow	cyan + magenta	yellow
cyan	yellow + magenta	cyan
magenta	yellow + cyan	magenta

FILTER CORRECTIONS PRINTING FROM SLIDES

Colour cast	Subtract	Or add
blue	cyan + magenta	yellow
green	yellow + cyan	magenta
red	yellow + magenta	cyan
yellow	yellow	cyan + magenta
cyan	cyan	yellow + magenta
magenta	magenta	yellow + cyan

INDEX

INDEX

Picture Credits

All photographs by the author except for the following:
Chris Bonington, page 155, bottom; Hugh Clark, page 147;
David Evans, page 95, bottom right; John Freeman, pages 92/
93, all except the top two pictures on page 92, and also page 136,
bottom picture; Jack Nisberg, page 26, bottom; John Salmon,
page 118. All pictures of cameras and equipment were shot by
the Longroom Studio.